CONTENTS

INTRODUCTION 4

MATERIALS 6

TECHNIQUES.................................... 8

Luna Lapin Comes Home 12

LUNA'S SAILOR COLLAR DRESS 14

Luna and the Washday Disaster 20

ROWAN'S WASHDAY APRON 22

Luna and the Windmill War 26

RAMSEY'S SHAWL COLLAR JUMPER .. 28

RAMSEY'S CARGO PANTS 31

RAMSEY'S BACKPACK 35

Luna Meets the Mayor 38

DAISY'S TWIRLING DRESS 40

Luna and the Salty Seadog 44

HUGH'S MATELOT TOP 46

HUGH'S BUTTON-FRONT TROUSERS 48

HUGH'S PEACOAT 52

HUGH'S BANDANA 59

Luna and the Unexpected Guest 60

FREYA'S HALTERNECK PLAYSUIT 62

FREYA'S OPERA COAT 67

FREYA'S MUSIC SATCHEL 72

How to Sew Luna and Friends 74

HOW TO MAKE LUNA 76

HOW TO MAKE HUGH 80

HOW TO MAKE ROWAN 86

HOW TO MAKE DAISY 92

HOW TO MAKE RAMSEY 99

HOW TO MAKE FREYA 101

THE PATTERNS 106

SUPPLIERS 142

ACKNOWLEDGEMENTS 142

ABOUT THE AUTHOR 142

INDEX 143

Introduction

Welcome to Luna Lapin's little world. Luna and all her friends are delighted to meet you. Inside these pages you will find easy to create characters and a wardrobe of beautiful, tiny tailored clothing. All of the clothes fit all of the animals (well, there might be a bit of tweaking for one huge fluffy tail, but let's not give Rowan Redtail a complex!).

If you are a long-standing Luna Lover, a heartfelt thank you from me and the team at CoolCrafting for all the support and encouragement you have shown this rabbity hare with her impeccable wardrobe and quiet, kind ways. Who would have thought that we would have reached a third book?

Luna is quite the celebrity in the crafting world and we like to think she is a byword for kindness. Luna is far more than a very sweet felt rabbit. She has become a conduit for friendships all over the world, and a whole community of creative stitchers have come together to offer advice and inspiration on our Facebook group, Luna Lapin's Little World.

This book is a doorway to creating your own heirlooms, whether they are close to our originals or adapted with your own quirks and variations. So, trust in me and enter a magical land of slowly stitched kindness and creativity.

Sarah
x

Materials

This section describes the materials and equipment you will need to make the projects in this book.

BASIC SEWING KIT

You will need some general supplies for making the projects in the book, including the following:

- Selection of needles, including sewing needle, tapestry needle, darner needle and doll needle (for sewing on arms)
- Sewing threads to suit projects, including embroidery threads
- Pins, safety pins and fabric clips
- Sharp scissors for fabric and scissors for paper
- Fabric marker (e.g. water-soluble pen or chalk)
- Adhesive tape (for joining pattern pieces)
- Turning tool for pushing out small shapes (if you don't own one, a knitting needle or chopstick will do)
- Iron and pressing cloth
- Sewing machine

BEFORE YOU START

Before starting a project, look at the You Will Need list for the project and gather your supplies. Give yourself enough space and time to work – this really does help eliminate mistakes. Read through all of a project's instructions first and highlight any areas that you will need to focus on more than the simpler parts. Press fabric with a suitable iron temperature to ensure it is flat and easy to work with (see Pressing Techniques).

FABRICS

Various fabric types have been used for the projects in the book and this section gives some advice on using them.

Felt

Felt is possibly the perfect crafting material. The felt I am referring to in this book is a flat fabric-like felt, not what you would use for needle-felting or wet felting. Felt is not a woven fabric, but is formed by the agitation of fibres and therefore will not fray when you cut it. This allows you to cut a shape that can be appliquéd, or sewn to the outside of a project. However, not all felts are made equal, so if possible choose a felt that has wool in it, and look for a thickness of about 1.5mm ($\frac{1}{16}$in) – definitely no thicker. I adore the softly marled tones of the felts that are used for Luna and her friends, which are a wool and rayon blend (see Suppliers). Felt doesn't have a grain to the material, so you can move your pattern pieces around to get the most out of your felt.

Corduroy

Corduroy is a fabric that has a luxurious look and feel. The fabric is made up of ribs of tufted fibres, called wales. Colours seem to glow in corduroy; think of it as a practical, everyday velvet. As with all of Luna and her friends' projects, it's important to think of their scaled down world, so choose a fine needlecord (one that has 14 wales per inch – or higher).

Printed Fabrics

Cotton tends to be more stable than other fabric compositions and therefore will give you more control when you are sewing these small items. Choose prints that work with the scale of the garment – that's why I love the ditsy prints you will see in some of the projects. Choose fabrics that are lightweight without being delicate – a quilting weight is about as heavy as you should select.

Knitted and Jersey Fabrics

This category encompasses a huge number of fabric types that share a common characteristic – they stretch, ideal for making simple over-the-head tops for our small friends, such as Hugh's matelot top. If this is your first time using stretch fabrics, try cutting up an old T-shirt to have a go.

When cutting out knitted or jersey fabrics, the stretch needs to go across the pattern pieces. To maintain the stretch in the garment, use a small zigzag or stretch stitch. A ballpoint or jersey needle prevents fibre damage and laddering but is not essential for such small garments. The nature of the fabric means seams do not need to be finished or pressed flat.

Velvet

Velvet, like corduroy, has a 'pile' but the even cut of this woven tufted fabric creates a flat, smooth surface. Velvet has a soft feel and a beautiful glow, making colours look even richer. It works well in loose, softly gathered shapes such as Freya's opera coat, but I wouldn't advise its use for small-scale garments that have a lot of detail.

Velvet has a tendency to shift and creep under your machine foot, so always prepare your seams well with tacking (basting). Changing the pressure on your machine foot will also help cope with this bulkier fabric. Velvet can be quite springy, so don't worry too much about pressing, and if you do need to press, use a scrap piece of velvet pile-side down as a pressing cloth.

Taffeta

Taffeta is a smooth surfaced cloth often associated with occasionwear. Very often it is woven with two different coloured threads (shot taffeta), resulting in a material that changes colour depending on angle or light, so it is important to be careful to keep your right and wrong sides consistent.

Be prepared for taffeta to shift as you cut and sew it, because of its smooth surface. Use a nice sharp needle on your machine, a little finer than normal (60–80 range) and do overlock or zigzag stitch your cut edges as this fabric frays easily.

Faux Leather / Pleather

These leather-look fabrics have a smooth surface that is slightly tacky to the touch. Made from a polyurethane surface bonded to a woven fabric back, faux leather (also called pleather) is an economical, vegan-friendly alternative to leather. (For a plastic-free alternative, look out for pinatex, a faux leather made from waste pineapple leaves.) Because the top layer on faux leather is not woven, the edges of this fabric won't fray, making it perfect for small accessories for Luna and her friends – boots, shoes and even tiny backpacks.

When working with faux leather, avoid using pins, or use them very carefully (i.e. within the seam allowance), as they will make permanently visible holes. Use a pen to draw around your pattern pieces onto the wrong side of the single layer fabric and transfer all markings in the same way. When sewing, you can use fabric clips to hold the parts together, and a non-stick Teflon foot will help the fabric to glide through the machine. Always try to sew on the back of the fabric, but if sewing on the right side, a little talcum powder on the surface will counteract the stickiness.

Faux Fur

Imitation fur comes in many different pile lengths and we have chosen a bushy variety to make Rowan's tail look rather impressive. We have chosen a tipped colourway for a more natural look.

When cutting out faux fur, snip the backing fabric only and then pull the shapes apart to minimise floating fibres. When sewing, changing the pressure on your machine foot will help cope with this bulkier fabric. When you have sewn your seams, use a comb or a strong pin to tease the fibres out of the seam.

Techniques

This section describes the basic techniques used for the projects. Each project is given a difficulty rating with the You Will Need lists – one balloon for easy projects, working up to three balloons for more difficult ones.

LAYOUTS

Layout diagrams are given for the projects as a guide for the amount of fabric needed, but if you have a different shape of fabric you will need to be flexible. Take note of which pattern piece will need to be cut out more than once and pin this onto double thickness fabric. The pattern pieces and layouts give this information so follow them carefully.

PATTERNS

All patterns are supplied full size in a section at the back of the book called The Patterns. Please follow the guidelines there for using the patterns.

CUTTING OUT

Time spent on accurate cutting will really improve your end result. Use a good quality pair of scissors that are suitable for (and reserved for) fabric. I tend to use the part of the blades that are closer to my hand to start cutting – this gives me better control and allows me to make a longer cut, as I have the rest of the blades to travel through the fabric. I only use the tips of the scissors when I am marking notches or for really fiddly bits.

TRANSFERRING MARKINGS

Mark the notches shown on the patterns with either a tiny snip in the fabric or using a water-soluble pen or chalk marker. Mark any triangles with a tiny snip at the centre. Mark any dots on the patterns with either a water-soluble pen or tailor's tacks. The triangles and dots are position markers. The notches can be there to mark a position or to help you ease around curves so please be accurate when you are snipping them. Once you have marked the positions, unpin the pattern pieces from the cut fabric and store them together once you are sure you have cut them all out.

RIGHT SIDE AND WRONG SIDE

Printed fabrics and some plain fabrics have a right side and a wrong side, and this is shown in the illustrations and referred to in the instructions. Felt normally has no definite right or wrong side, but I have referred to right and wrong to help you sew.

FINISHING RAW EDGES

You could use an overlocker or a machine zigzag stitch to finish the raw edges of the seams on woven fabrics. The items in this book are small ones that are not going to be washed, so this is optional. Because of the nature of felt, the edges do not need finishing.

HAND SEWING STITCHES

Hand sewing is relaxing, portable and allows you to focus on something creative. Luna's friends are sewn by hand and you could aim to complete a limb each night or perhaps take her on your commute to work. I have used various stitches, both practical and pretty. Always start and finish with either a knot in the fabric or a couple of small stitches in the same place.

Overstitch / Whipstitch

I use an overstitch (also called whipstitch) to sew felt pieces together. Use a single thread thickness and make sure you sew consistently, that is, the same distance between stitches and the same depth in from the edge, about 2mm ($\frac{1}{16}$in) into the felt.

Bring the needle through to the front and then sew from back to front, repeating and working from right to left if you are right-handed (see **Fig.1**) or left to right if you are left-handed. As you pull the thread through you will feel the tension as the thread is drawn and you can then continue to the next stitch. The thread will sink into the felt.

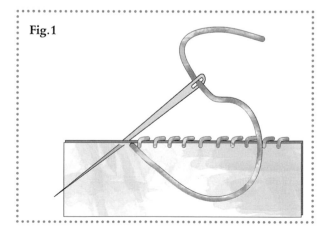

Fig.1

Backstitch

Backstitch is used to sew two pieces of fabric or felt together with a seam allowance. Backstitch is a good replacement for machine sewing if you wish to sew the garments by hand. Use a single toning sewing thread on your needle.

Following **Fig.2**, bring the needle up at point 1 and then back to point 2. Bring it out at the top again beyond point 1 at point 3, and then back through at point 4, which should be very close to or in the same place as point 1. Repeat along the seam.

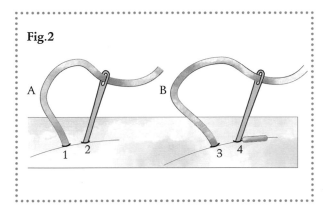

Fig.2

Blanket Stitch

Blanket stitch is a decorative and functional stitch that can be used to make a seam and to decorate it at the same time. The key to a good blanket stitch is consistency in the depth of the stitch and the distance between the stitches. A common mistake is to make the stitch too close to the edge of the fabric, which loses the decorative quality. Use a contrast embroidery thread to work blanket stitch – I tend to use between three and six strands of embroidery thread, depending on how bold I want the contrast stitch to look.

Following **Fig.3**, bring the needle through to the front at point 1.Insert the needle in the front at point 2 and come out at the back at point 3, holding the thread under the needle at point 3 as you pull the stitch tight.

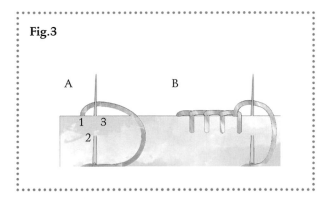

Fig.3

Satin Stitch

Satin stitch is an embroidery stitch that is good for creating blocked-out shapes in contrast colours. Use between three and six strands of the embroidery thread, depending on how bold you want the contrast stitch to look.

Following **Fig.4**, draw out the outline of the shape you are going to fill. Use the needle to pass backwards and forwards from outline to opposite outline. Try to keep your stitches parallel to one another and don't pull the stitches too tight.

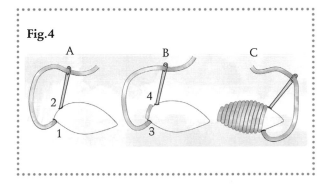

Fig.4

Slip Stitch / Ladder Stitch

A slip stitch (also called ladder stitch) is used to join two fabrics when you don't want the stitches to show. Following **Fig.5**, secure the thread onto a bulkier part of the project – a seam allowance or the fold of a hem. Now pass your needle through a tiny amount of the main fabric and then travel diagonally into the back of the other fabric piece. Come down directly into the main fabric again, pick up a small amount again and travel diagonally across to the second fabric again. Repeat along the edge.

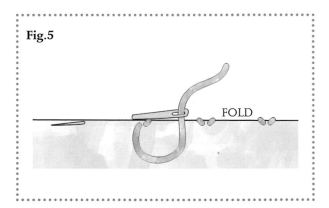

Fig.5

FOLD

MACHINE SEWING TECHNIQUES

I recommend sewing the clothes for Luna and her friends on a sewing machine as this will give a more professional and even finish. For these projects it is assumed that you have the basic skills of machine sewing. However, here are a few tips on how to sew small items.

The Right Stitch

Test your fabrics first, for example, a cotton lawn will react differently to a faux fur under the machine and you may need to adjust the stitch length or tension.

'Donkey' or Stitch Starter

If you find that with small projects and fine fabrics your fabric tends to disappear down into the needle plate at the start of a seam, you could use what's called a donkey. Fold over a piece of scrap fabric so it's about 5cm (2in) square and a few layers thick and start your line of sewing on this. Butt the project up to the donkey and continue sewing onto the project – reversing as in Securing Your Stitching, below, but without involving the donkey. You can snip the threads to detach the donkey at the end of the seam and use it again and again.

Securing Your Stitching

Always use your machine reverse function to start and finish seams as this will stop your seams from coming undone. The reversing should only be for two to three stitches – if you stitch any more than this then you probably will have lost the line of stitching anyway.

Seam Allowance

It is amazing how many people come to my Make Friends with Your Sewing Machine classes who don't know what the little parallel grooves are on the footplate of the sewing machine. These are your sewing guidelines and before you start sewing you should identify which line is right for the recommended seam allowance. So, if sewing with a 1cm (⅜in) seam allowance, you should be feeding the sewing through the machine so the raw edges are on the right-hand side of the presser foot and are running along the 10mm groove. If you are working to a narrow 0.5cm (¼in) seam allowance, use the edge of your presser foot as the guide for the edge of the fabric.

Using the Hand Wheel

Instead of using the foot pedal, using your hand wheel to make the last few stitches before a point you are aiming for can really improve your accuracy and confidence. Always turn the wheel towards you.

Turning a Corner

To make a crisp, accurate 90-degree corner when you are sewing, at the point of the corner leave the needle down in the fabric, lift the presser foot and move the fabric around at a 90-degree angle, and then continue sewing.

Coping with Curves

Sewing a curve is easier if you are using your seam guidelines. Slow down to control your sewing more easily and if you need to realign what you are doing, leave the needle down in the fabric, lift the presser foot and move the fabric slightly to bring the curve back in line. You may find that you have a speed setting on your machine or foot pedal, so if it helps you should slow the speed down whilst you practise new techniques. A needle down function on your machine is invaluable for working on curves such as when inserting sleeves into a garment.

Easing

There are times when it feels like you are squeezing more fabric on one side to match less fabric on another side. This can occur, for example, if you are setting in a sleeve or sewing a curve onto a straight piece of fabric. To help with easing there are two different techniques, as follows.

METHOD 1

This is the normal dressmaking technique. Change your stitch length to be the longest possible. Do not reverse at the beginning or end, and then on the longer looking side (normally the curved side), sew two rows of stitching. Row 1 should be 3mm (⅛in) from the raw edge. Row 2 should be 6mm (¼in). Now grab the sewing threads from one end of the upper side of the fabric and gently pull to slightly gather up the fabric. Do the same with the other ends, but make sure you don't have actual gathers, just more tightness. Now you can pin and sew to the other piece of fabric and eventually remove the initial stitching. Remember to change your stitch length back to normal first though.

METHOD 2

This is the factory method. Take the tighter (usually the straighter piece of fabric) and put snips 1cm (⅜in) apart along the edge of the fabric, which are a little bit shorter than the seam allowance allowed. This will lengthen the edge of the fabric and allow it to stretch to the longer curved piece.

Staystitching

Staystitching is a foundation step to keep your fabric from stretching. Sew using a normal length straight stitch just inside the given seam allowance so that your stitches will be hidden. Sew without reversing at the beginning or end of your sewing so that you can easily remove the stitches if necessary.

Edgestitch

An edgestitch is a line of stitching that is very close, about 1mm–2mm (1/32in–1/16in) away from a seam or folded edge. It is used to decorate or strengthen a seam. An easy way of establishing a guideline for edgestitching is to move your needle across to the left-hand position and then use the groove in the centre of the presser foot as your seam guideline. Stitch slowly to keep the stitching even.

Topstitch

A topstitch is a line of stitching that is close, about 4mm–5mm (3/16in) away from a seam or folded edge. It is used to decorate or strengthen a seam. Use the edge of the presser foot as your seam guideline. Edgestitching and topstitching can be used together to create a twin needling effect.

Gathering

Gathering is a decorative effect, allowing a longer piece of fabric to be suppressed into a shorter piece of fabric. It creates a pretty effect and can create shaping in a garment.

To gather, change your machine stitch to be at its longest, or to the gathering setting. Following **Fig.6**, sew along the top edge 0.5cm (1/4in) down and then repeat the line of stitching 1cm (3/8in) down. This standard spacing between lines of gathering may vary depending on the outfit and any variation is given in the instructions. It is important that you don't reverse or fasten your threads off at this stage. Take the two top threads from one end (tying them to one another helps) and firmly but steadily pull the threads so the material moves along and gathers. Repeat with the top threads at the other end and gather up the fabric to the specified length. Tie off the ends of the thread to secure the gathering or wind in a figure of eight around a pin. I cannot stress enough how valuable it is to spend time getting your gathers evenly distributed along the fabric. When you have sewn the fabrics together as instructed for each garment, the original gathering threads can be pulled out.

Making Buttonholes

Buttonholes are a finishing touch to garments and an important fastening function BUT in this tiny world, it might be difficult for your sewing machine to create buttonholes. So have a think about your capabilities, practise on your machine with some scrap fabric and most importantly, remember it would be a horrible thing to have got almost to the end of making the clothes to then make a mess of the buttonholes.

If you are having a go, a sewing machine with either a computerised function (where you can put in the length of buttonhole required) will work, as will machines where you turn a knob for each stage of the buttonhole. A machine which has a foot where the button drops into the back to determine the buttonhole length will not work – the button is too small to be detected. Once the buttonhole is completed, cut through the small area between the zigzag stitches carefully using an unpicker. To do this safely, place pins at each far end of the buttonhole, but just before the wide end bar of stitching. This will stop the unpicker from accidentally cutting further.

If you don't want to try machine buttonholes, you could always embroider the detail on using a satin stitch, or just use buttons and snap fasteners.

PRESSING TECHNIQUES

An iron is as valuable to the sewing process as the sewing machine itself. Make sure you have a pressing cloth available to cover your project as you feel necessary. Keep scrap fabric to test the temperature and the use of steam before you work on your project. Some seams will be too small to press, but it's worth making the effort, depending on the shape, to set the seam first by pressing the seam flat. Then open up the fabric and use the nose of the iron to either open up the seam allowances and press flat.

If you are working on turning out a shape like Luna's sailor collar for example, after trimming your seam allowances as per the instructions, turn through and use your thumb and fingers to roll the seam right out onto the edge of the shape before pressing with the iron.

Throughout the pressing process, your fingers will be working near the hot iron, so do take care.

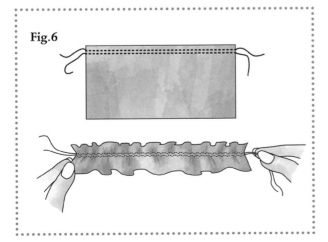

Fig.6

Luna Lapin COMES home

Luna waited nervously at the front door of the burrow she had spent many happy years in as a young rabbit. The house didn't seem that different from the outside but there was a general feeling of age that made the corners a little fuzzy, be it the dust and webs gathering in the corners of the white wood window frames or the lawn that wasn't quite as well manicured as it used to be, little tufts of grass sticking up here and there. Luna opened the heavy door and stepped inside the burrow. It smelled exactly the same as it always had: of warmth; old books; and slightly sweet as if a cake was cooling uncovered on the kitchen worktop.

"I'm in the sitting room," a familiar voice said.

Luna's granny was sitting in her usual spot on the sofa under the window. The pile of books and newspapers to her left was, as usual, topped by a cup of tea, her knitting was set aside to her right. Luna beamed down at her. Luna Lapin was a quiet and kind rabbit, and she was not at all the kind of rabbit that had favourites. She was just as charming and good natured to anyone she met, but if, at a pinch, she was made to pick someone out as her favourite she would most definitely pick her granny.

Granny had always been her biggest inspiration and the rabbit that believed in her most. Granny was always the first to say "You can do this," or "Look at you go Luna!" or "Luna Lapin, you are the most special rabbit," whenever it needed saying. Granny had been the person who had bought her a painting set when she was six and told her she was good enough to be an illustrator some day. Granny had taught her to sew her own clothes and taught her good manners. Without Granny Luna would never have been brave enough to follow her dream to move from her sleepy little home to the big city. Granny was Luna's very best friend in the whole wide world and Luna would do anything to make her proud.

Luna thought about the beautiful patchwork scarf Granny had gifted her all those years ago and how she still carried its good luck with her. Granny's house had always been a special place for Luna growing up; it was filled with books and treasures, stories and memories.

Luna felt guilty that she hadn't been able to visit her granny more over the past couple of years but things had just been so busy at work: she was a fashion designer now, a breakout star in the industry.

Luna glanced at the rabbit she looked up to so much and for the first time noticed how much smaller she seemed. Granny's little gold-rimmed glasses were perched on the end of her nose as they always were, a pale pink cardigan draped around her shoulders. Granny's face was speckled grey and her memories had settled into her face. Luna thought about how this was the first time she hadn't been greeted at the door with a warm smile and a "Now, would you like a cup of tea?" Luna felt so terribly sad that there was nothing she could do to help, other than to fetch them both a slice of cake.

Whilst Granny and Luna talked and ate, it became clear to Luna that Granny was lonely. She was still the same kind-hearted Granny as ever, but her stories were much older than Luna was used to. In past visits Granny had been full of stories about lunches with friends, and charity galas, garden parties and bargain hunting at antiques fairs. Granny told Luna that she hadn't been getting out of the house quite as much. Luna decided that she would throw her a party, a party with music and old friends and good food and laughter. Granny was turning 80 in three moons and that gave Luna just enough time to plan. Luna was going to need help if she could pull this off and she knew exactly who to call… After all, you are never too old to make new stories.

Luna's Sailor
Collar Dress

YOU WILL NEED

- **One fat quarter of striped quilting weight 100% cotton fabric for main fabric**
- **40cm (16in) x 20cm (8in) contrast quilting weight 100% cotton fabric for collar**
- **Five 6mm (¼in) buttons**
- **Five press studs**
- **50cm (20in) of 6mm (¼in) ribbon trim**
- **Basic sewing kit (see Materials)**

Use a 0.5cm (¼in) seam allowance, unless a different amount is stated.

CUTTING OUT

1 Fold the striped fabric in half with right sides together. Pin your cut-out pattern pieces (see Patterns) onto the fabric using **Fig.1** as a guide. Cut all pieces as stated on the pattern. Mark any notches with a small snip, including an 'on the fold' snip to mark the centre point of the skirt and back pieces. Transfer any other pattern markings to the fabric.

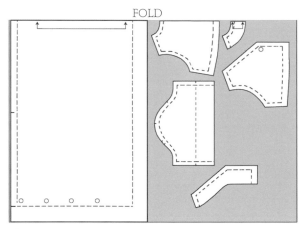

Fig.1

2 Fold the contrast fabric in half with right sides together. Pin on the collar pattern piece and cut out. Mark all notches with a small snip.

MAKING UP

Making the Collar

1 With right sides together, match and pin the two collar pieces. Sew around the outside edges of the collar, starting at one notch and finishing at the opposite notch as shown in **Fig.2**, working carefully around the curves and pivoting to turn corners (see Machine Sewing Techniques: Turning a Corner). Trim excess seam allowance away at corners and points and snip into the inner corners where you started and finished stitching.

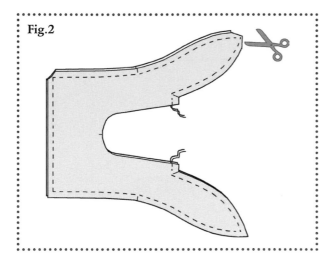

Fig.2

2 Turn the collar through to the right side, then use a knitting needle or similar to push out the points (**Fig.3**). Roll the seams out to the edge and press flat (see Techniques: Pressing).

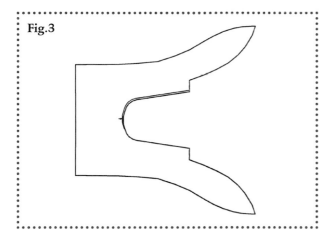

Fig.3

Sewing the Shoulder Seams

1 With right sides together, match and pin one front shoulder seam to one back shoulder seam, then sew together.

2 Repeat to sew the remaining front piece to the back at the shoulder seam (**Fig.4**). Press seams open.

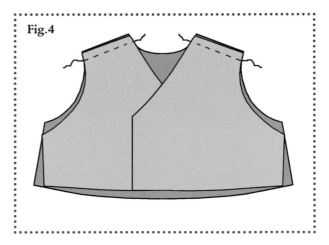

Fig.4

Sewing the Facing Shoulder Seams

1 With right sides together, match and pin one front facing shoulder seam to one back facing shoulder seam, then sew together.

2 Repeat to sew the remaining front facing piece to the back facing at the shoulder seam (**Fig.5**). Press seams open and finish the outside edge using an overlocker or zigzag stitch (**Fig.6**).

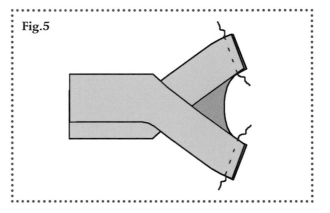

Fig.5

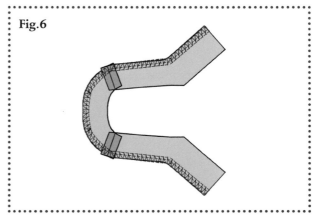

Fig.6

Sewing the Collar to the Dress

1 With the joined back/fronts right side up, position the best side of the collar upward (**Fig.7**), matching the notches at the neckline. Pin, then tack (baste) in place.

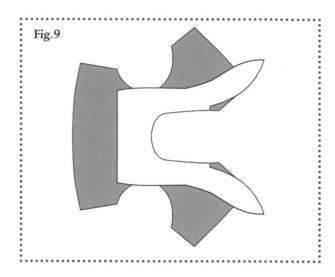

Fig.9

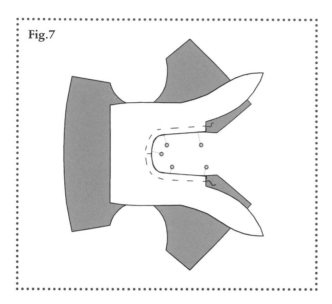

Fig.7

2 Now place the joined facing on top right side down, carefully matching at the neckline and at the front edge of the bodice, and pin in place. Starting from the lower edge of one front, sew around the neckline to finish at the lower edge of the other front. Snip into the seam allowance at the neck curve to ensure it sits flat once turned. Trim the excess from the corner angles (**Fig.8**). Turn the facing to the inside and press the neckline and front edges flat (**Fig.9**).

Making and Attaching the Sleeves

1 Finish the raw edges of the sleeve hems using an overlocker or zigzag stitch. Press to the wrong side at the notches to create a deep hem on each sleeve and edgestitch in place (**Fig.10**).

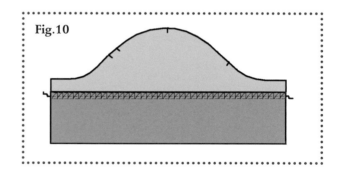

Fig.10

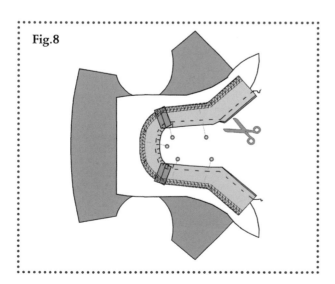

Fig.8

2 With sleeves right side facing up, fold and press a 1cm (⅜in) deep cuff on each (**Fig.11**). Check that you have made two mirror image sleeves.

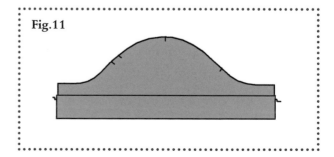

Fig.11

3 With right sides together, match one sleeve to an armhole using the notches to position and to ensure you have the correct sleeve in the correct armhole. Pin in place and sew.

4 Repeat with the other sleeve and armhole. Press seams towards body and use an overlocker or zigzag stitch to finish (**Fig.12**).

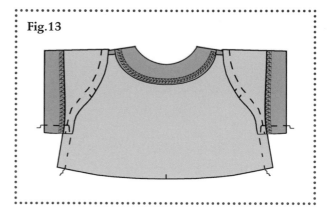

Fig.13

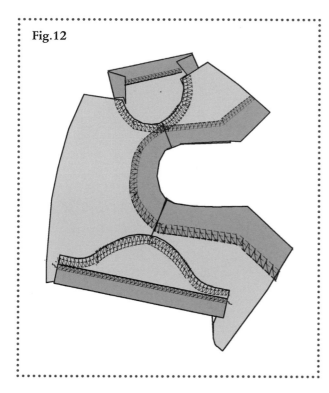

Fig.12

Gathering the Skirt

1 Take your skirt piece and finish the short edges using an overlocker or zigzag stitch. Starting and finishing at the centre front notches, sew lines of gathering stitch along the top edge (see Machine Sewing Techniques: Gathering).

2 Gather up the top threads, first from one end then the other, until the waistline of the skirt roughly measures the same as that of the bodice. Ensure that the ends of the gathered threads remain visible and usable (**Fig.14**).

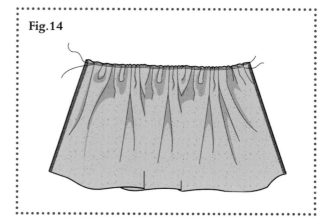

Fig.14

Sewing the Underarm and Side Seams of the Bodice

1 Check on the right side of the sleeves that the cuffs are still folded back correctly and adjust if necessary.

2 With right sides together, match and pin the underarm seams and the side seams of the bodice. Starting at the edge of the sleeve, sew in place, pivoting at the underarm (**Fig.13**) (note that for clarity we have left the overlock stich off the sleeve seams in this diagram so that you can see the pivot point). Finish the underarm seams and the side seams using an overlocker or zigzag stitch.

Attaching the Skirt to the Bodice

1 With right sides together, match the gathered top of the skirt to the bodice, matching centre back and side seam notches. The front notches will match up with the front seam.

2 Adjust your gathers to be even, then sew skirt and bodice together using a 1cm (⅜in) seam allowance (**Fig.15**). I normally like to sew with my gathers upwards, so I can better see to avoid catching the lower skirt in the seam. Remove any visible threads from the gathering stage.

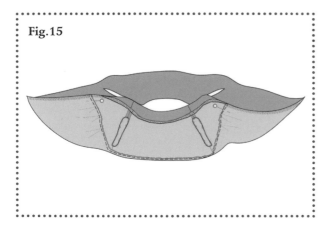

Fig.15

3 Finish the waist seam using an overlocker or zigzag stitch. Re-fold the bodice front facing to the inside and press the skirt edge in by the same amount (2cm/¾in) to create the skirt front facing. Press the seam allowance towards the bodice.

Sewing the Hem

1 The intended hem is 2cm (¾in) deep. Fold the skirt facings back on themselves – so right sides are together. Sew across this turning at the depth of the hem (**Fig.16**). Trim off the corner excess and cut the facing seam allowance back.

2 Press the rest of the hem up by 2cm (¾in) and sew in place 1.5cm (⅝in) up from the folded edge.

Fig.16

FINISHING OFF

1 Cover the hem stitching line with the satin ribbon trim. Edgestitch in place along each side of the ribbon and tuck under a small amount at the front edges for a neat finish (**Fig.17**).

Fig.17

2 Use the marked positions to sew the buttons onto the right-hand side (as worn) of the dress front, one on the bodice and four on the skirt. (I chose an alternative colour for one of my buttons for a jaunty designer feel.) Beneath each button, sew a press stud on the wrong side of the fabric. Then sew the other half of each press stud on the left-hand side (as worn).

3 To make a fabric toggle to pass the ends of the collar through when the dress is being worn, cut a piece of striped fabric 3cm (1⅛in) x 1.5cm (⅝in). Fold into three along the length and then sew through all layers. Fold the toggle in half so that the short ends meet and sew with a 0.5cm (¼in) seam allowance (**Fig.18**). Trim the seam allowance and turn through to the right side.

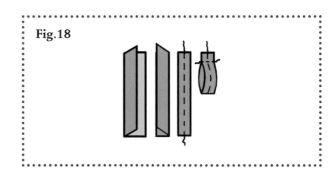

Fig.18

Luna
AND THE WASHDAY
disaster

Rowan Redtail was full of mischief. Surefooted and agile, Rowan had considered a career as a professional pickpocket because she was so nimble but had settled on being a tree surgeon instead. This suited her just as well and kept her on the right side of the law.

Rowan lived deep in the Lake District in a treehouse with green blinds that let natural light seep in and kiss every woody corner. Her fruit bowl was always full but her bed was never made, Rowan had far too much to do to worry about things like that. Rowan couldn't be prouder of her little home: she had only finished building it a year ago and on warm nights it still smelled of fresh timber.

"Luna!" Rowan called as the little grey rabbit made her way up the path. "You're early." Luna wasn't early, Rowan just did everything in her own time and in her own way. The squirrel's tufted ears twitched in excitement, tail bobbing behind her as she wrestled with the sheet she held. Rowan was wearing nothing but a washday apron and was hanging the rest of her clothes between the branches of the trees! Luna chuckled to herself, it was so lovely to see that her old friend hadn't changed at all.

"Hope you don't mind heights," chirped the squirrel as she pointed to the ladder. Luna stared at the ladder with apprehension; rabbits were definitely not made for climbing and, to be honest, she was afraid of heights. Luna had never joined in with Alfie and Rowan as they scrambled their way through their childhood, preferring instead the feel of a needle and thread at her fingers, and grass under her feet. Luna didn't know where her fear came from, but she did know that she was struck with panic at the top of every balcony she encountered. The hot bubble of fear rose from her toes to her ear tips as she looked up at the treehouse and she shuddered as she imagined the view from the top.

"Actually, I need to head down," said Rowan. Luna exhaled: she would have to make her way up the ladder eventually, but for now she could relax. Rowan slid down the side of the ladder holding a flask, a basket of apples and a Battenberg cake. Everything Rowan did was done at speed and with enthusiasm. Luna loved this about her friend. Who better to help her find Granny's friends than this curious, twitchy squirrel.

They sat and talked about their plans for what seemed like minutes but was really hours. Rowan's nose started to twitch

"Can you smell that?" she asked Luna. Luna could smell the earthy ground and the sticky marzipan, she could smell the crispness of the apples, and the faint scent of wild garlic, but she couldn't smell whatever that was. "It's about to rain! You really are a city dweller now, Luna Lapin," Rowan teased, scarpering up the ladder, shouting something about her washing.

Rain began to fall heavily and the canopy came alive with the sound of raindrops hitting leaves but Luna didn't move from the bottom of the ladder. She couldn't bring herself to step onto the first rung of the ladder never mind the third or thirtieth. It was too high. What if she fell? What if it was too slippery? So many what ifs …

Luna heard a cry. A sheet drifted down through the air, landing over Luna's head. Luna scrambled to get out from under it but every time she moved it became more twisted. All she could hear were her friend's cries for help! Luna pulled the sheet this way and that, becoming more frightened for her friend. Finally free, Luna looked up and saw Rowan, precariously balanced on the edge of the balcony.

"I'm slipping, help!" she cried, losing her footing.

"I'm coming!" shouted Luna, but she couldn't move. Luna was terrified of the ladder and for her friend. "Come on Luna" she whispered to herself, staring not at the red squirrel but at the formidable ladder. Granny's voice sounded in her head. "You can do this, my brave little rabbit. Paw and then foot. Don't look down. You are as brave as you are kind, you can do this."

Luna followed her granny's advice; she could do this.

"Luna, quick!"

Rowan was caught on a branch by the crisscross of her vintage apron. Luna rushed towards her, grabbing Rowan by the tail. Squirrels hate it when you touch their tails but this was an exceptional circumstance. Luna pulled Rowan backwards and they collapsed together against the wall of the treehouse panting from different kinds of fear.

"That was close, I thought you weren't going to make it in time. Thank goodness you did," cried Rowan.

"Neither did I! I am sorry but I'm terrified of heights," Luna admitted. She didn't know why she hadn't just talked about her worry earlier. It is always better to be honest with your friends about your feelings.

Rowan's Washday Apron

YOU WILL NEED

- **40cm (16in) x 110cm (45in) of light to quilting weight 100% cotton or linen blend fabric***
- **Basic sewing kit (see Materials)**

Use a 0.5cm (¼in) seam allowance, unless a different amount is stated.

*If you choose to have a different fabric for the lining, use two complementary fat quarters.

CUTTING OUT

1 With wrong side facing upwards, fold the selvedges in to meet in the middle to give you two folded edges. Now you will be laying out your pattern pieces onto the right side of the fabric. Pin your cut-out pattern pieces (see Patterns) onto the fabric using **Fig.1** as a guide. (If using different fabrics for the outer and the lining, fold each fat quarter in half right sides together and make sure to place the main body pattern up against the fold.) Cut all pieces as stated on the pattern: note that the pocket pattern should be cut from just a single layer of fabric. Mark any triangles with a small snip to the centre and mark any notches with a small snip. Transfer any other pattern markings to the fabric.

Fig.1

MAKING UP

Making and Attaching the Pockets

1 With right sides together, fold the pocket piece down at the side notches, matching the edges. Starting at the folded edge and using a 1cm (³⁄₈in) seam allowance, sew to the first notch, then leave a gap and resume sewing from the second notch back up to the folded edge taking your time around the curves (**Fig.2**).

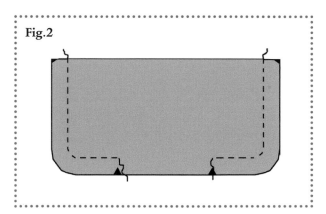

Fig.2

2 Trim off the excess at the top corners and notch the seam allowances around the curves to reduce bulk. Turn the pocket through to the right side using the opening, pushing out the corners. Press the seam allowance inwards and close the opening with slip stitch (see Hand Sewing Techniques: Slip Stitch).

3 To make the pocket pleat, fold the pocket in half widthways and sew a short line of stitching (approx. 1.5cm/ ⅝in) down from the top edge, working 0.5cm (¼in) from the folded edge (**Fig.3**). Press the pleat flat at the back (**Fig.4**).

Fig.3

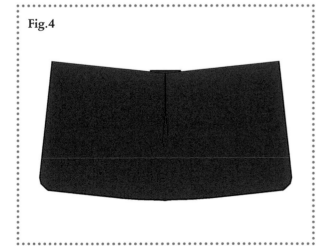

Fig.4

4 Position the pocket onto the right side of the outer fabric of the main body. Pin in place, then sew using an edgestitch (see Machine Sewing Techniques: Edgestitch), leaving the top edge free (**Fig.5**).

Fig.5

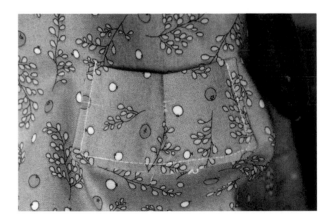

Sewing the Main Body

1 With right sides together, match the outer to the lining around all edges and pin.

2 Starting just in from the corner at the lower back edge (see **Fig.6**), sew all the way up to the top of the strap. Leaving the top of the strap open, resume sewing from the other side of the strap and continue around the armhole curve, stopping when you get to the top edge. Leaving the top edge open, resume sewing from the other side, around the armhole curve to the top of the second strap.

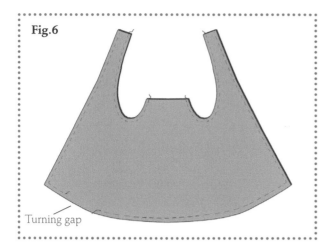

Fig.6

Turning gap

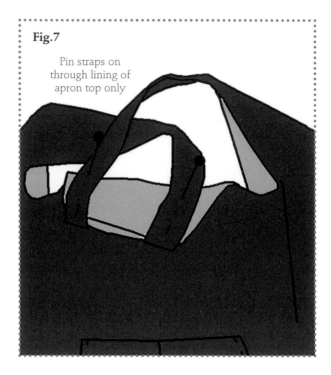

Fig.7

Pin straps on
through lining of
apron top only

3 Leaving the top of the second strap open, resume sewing from the other side of the strap, heading down to the lower back corner and continuing all the way around the hem to within 6cm (2³/₈in) of where you started to allow for a turning gap as seen in **Fig.6**. Trim off any excess seam allowance at the corners and snip into the curves.

4 Turn the apron through to the right side, rolling the seams to the edge between your fingers and thumbs. Make sure the straps are pushed fully out and press flat. Do not close the turning gap yet.

Attaching the Straps to the Apron Top

1 This part of the construction can be a little tricky so take your time. First, with the pocket side of the apron facing upwards, fold the outer part of the apron down so you can see the lining side. Take the left-hand strap and bring it over to the right-hand side of the apron top without twisting it and pin it onto the lining fabric only, matching the strap to the outside edges. Now bring the right-hand strap over to the left-hand side of the apron top, again without twisting it, and pin it onto the lining fabric only, matching the strap to the outside edges as before (**Fig.7**). Note that the straps should extend just a little further than the edge of the apron top. Before moving on to the next step, take the time to make sure that the edges of the straps are lined up with the outside edges of the apron top and check that you have not pinned through both layers but through the lining fabric only. If you like, you can tack (baste) the straps in place and remove the pins.

2 Use the opening at the bottom hem to turn the apron (or at least the top part of it) inside out again. Smooth out the edge of the apron top, making sure that the front and back edges (which have the straps sandwiched in between) are matching. The ends of the straps should stand a little proud to ensure that they will be caught in the seam. Once you are happy, sew across the top edge (**Fig.8**).

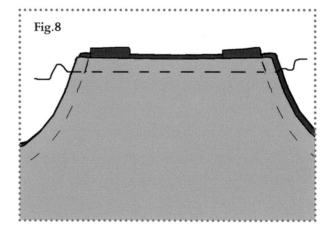

Fig.8

FINISHING OFF

1 Turn the apron through to the right side once more and sew up the opening in the hem, enclosing the seam allowances, using slip stitch or ladder stitch (see Hand Sewing Stitches).

Luna
AND THE
windmill war

Luna woke to the sounds of chirping outside, the treehouse was warm and Rowan Redtail had already gone out. Luna wasn't exactly sure where Rowan disappeared to in the morning but she always returned with something exciting. Freddie was due to arrive soon and Luna couldn't wait to introduce her friends. She was looking forward to the two of them talking about wildlife, their favourite types of tree and debating the best way of growing lettuce.

Luna hadn't seen Freddie in weeks and was eager to update him on what she was planning for her granny's 80th birthday. From the balcony of the treehouse Luna could see his old Land Rover coming towards them.

Rowan snuck up behind her. "Is that him?", she asked. Luna jumped! "Please stop doing that, I'm still scared of heights you know!"

"Sorry," said Rowan. "I'm overexcited! I can't believe we are really going to track down your granny's old friends – she will love this. Have you had any replies to your letters? Where shall we go first? Oh look! He is here!"

Rowan sped down the ladder. "Oh gosh," thought Luna, "Rowan will have talked his ears off by the time I get down!"

Freddie, the softly spoken badger, and the silly chattering squirrel got on like a house on fire. The trio made a plan to visit Daisy, the proud Herdwick from Granny's teenage years.

Daisy lived in a small village in the Lakes with narrow streets and knobbly grey stone houses. A river ran through the middle and the town was a maze of yards and tiny shops. Luna looked forward to seeing Daisy after all these years and hoped there was more she could learn from the clever Herdwick.

The day opened crisp and bright, Freddie and Rowan agreed it certainly didn't feel like rain, Luna didn't say anything for fear they would tease her about being a city rabbit. No one answered at Daisy's cottage so they decided to make the most of the good weather and headed through the steep streets that wrapped the hillside. Soon the town was far behind them and there was nothing but lush fields that turned into fellside.

No one had noticed the dark clouds roll in.

"I thought you said it wasn't going to rain!" Luna cried rushing for cover. They were miles from town and didn't have a clue about the most direct route back. "I guess we just wait it out," said Freddie. Within minutes they were completely soaked.

Ramsey really disliked three things: bananas, climate change, and red skies in the morning. Not necessarily in that order. If he was to add a fourth it would be unprepared city folk ruining his walks with their lack of maps and decent footwear. Ramsey spotted the three tourists huddled up across the field and thought about turning around, hoping they hadn't seen him. It was too late, they were waving at him.

"Great," he thought, "just great, another perfectly fine walk ruined." If it carried on like this he might as well take up golf.

Luna, Rowan and Daisy stood miserably under the tree. Ramsey walked towards them grumbling about being unprepared for all weathers when walking. Freddie especially felt ashamed, he took great pride in being knowledgeable about the land and he was very disappointed that his weather prediction had failed him. Rowan as usual seemed unphased.

A flash of recognition shot through the stranger's eyes when Luna finally managed to stop looking down at her feet and explained what had happened.

"Luna Lapin! Lido hero! We will make an activist out of you yet," and his face lifted up into a smile. "Name's Ramsey, I'm from 'round corner here. Let's get you warmed up, see if we can get you back to your car."

Ramsey lived on a smallholding just outside town, the yard was full of scraps and he had a solar panelled roof.

"Oops, watch you don't step on that," he said, gesturing vaguely around. "Sorry about the mess, been busy with the campaign recently."

Ramsey made hot chocolate, and they settled in front of a tired looking Aga. Ramsey explained that he was currently having trouble with what felt like the whole town over a wind farm. He had offered some of his land to become a wind farm that would generate enough power for all the local schools, but the townsfolk kept objecting on the grounds that it would damage the views.

Ramsey kept telling them there would be no more views left if they did nothing about the climate crisis, but would they listen? Ramsey let out a downtrodden sigh. Until recently he had thought he was getting somewhere, especially with the mayor, but she wouldn't even let him speak at the last meeting. The mayor was a funny old ewe, he said, known her for years, never seen eye to eye, always going on about what was good for the townsfolk. Ramsey only cared about the planet as he had met enough folk to feel this way.

Ramsey's Shawl Collar Jumper

YOU WILL NEED

- **15cm (6in) x 70cm (27½in) knitted or jersey fabric**
- **Basic sewing kit (see Materials)**

Use a 0.5cm (¼in) seam allowance, unless a different amount is stated.

CUTTING OUT

1 With right side facing upwards, fold the short edges in to meet in towards the middle to give you two folded edges. Now you will be laying out your pattern pieces onto the wrong side of the fabric. Pin your cut-out pattern pieces (see Patterns) onto the fabric using **Fig.1** as a guide. Cut all pieces as stated on the pattern. Mark any notches with a small snip including an 'on the fold' snip to mark the centre back points on the collar and back pieces. Transfer any other pattern markings to the fabric.

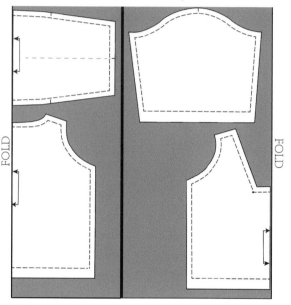

Fig.1

MAKING UP

Sewing the Shoulder Seams

1 With right sides together, match and pin the front and back shoulder seams, then sew (**Fig.2**).

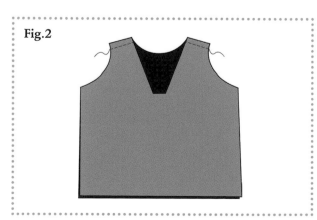

Fig.2

Sewing the Sleeves

1 Turn 1cm (³/₈in) to the wrong side of each sleeve hem and zigzag stitch in place, taking care not to stretch the fabric as you sew.

2 With right sides together, match and pin one sleeve onto each armhole and sew in place (**Fig.3**).

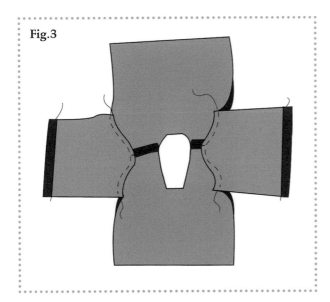

Fig.3

Making and Attaching the Shawl Collar

1 With wrong sides together, fold the shawl collar in half along the marked fold line and tack (baste) around the open edges (**Fig.4**). Make sure you have your dots marked for the next stage.

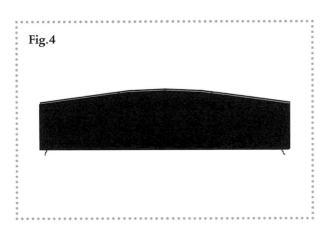

Fig.4

2 Using your notches, position the shawl collar onto the neckline, right sides together. Match the dots on the collar to the dots on the jumper front, to get the level right at the front lower neckline (see **Fig.5** and **Fig.6**). Sew around the neckline from dot to dot (**Fig.6**). (If you find this difficult, you can tackle the seam one half at a time starting at the centre back.)

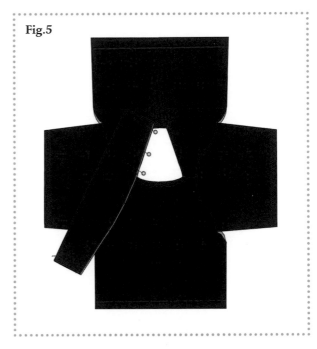

Fig.5

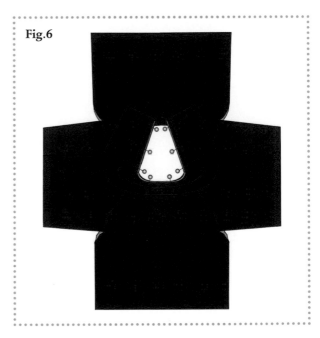

Fig.6

3 At the front lower collar, bring the folded edge of the right-hand collar (as worn) over to the left-hand dot, then take the folded edge of the left-hand collar (as worn) over to the right-hand dot (**Fig.7**).

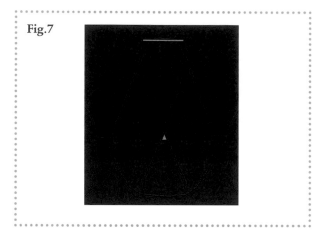

Fig.7

4 Turning to the wrong side, snip into the corners of the seam allowance up to the dots. Now fold the front of the jumper at the level of the dots, pushing the free ends of the collar to the wrong side, and level up with the lower collar edge on the front of the jumper. Sew across all layers (**Fig.8**) (when you turn through to the right side, this should be a nice horizontal seam).

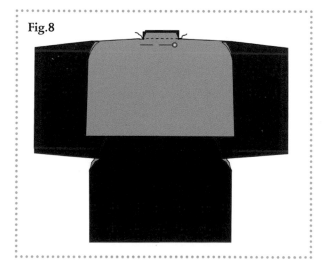

Fig.8

Sewing the Side Seams and Hem

1 With right sides together, match the underarms and body side seams, then sew.

2 At the hem, turn 1cm (³⁄₈in) to the wrong side and zigzag stitch in place, taking care not to stretch the fabric as you sew (**Fig.9**).

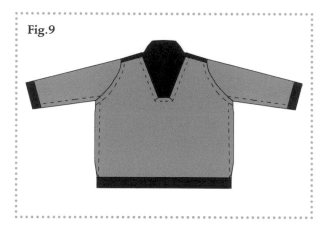

Fig.9

Ramsey's Cargo Pants

YOU WILL NEED

- **One fat quarter of fine needlecord for main fabric**
- **10cm (4in) of cotton lawn fabric for pocket bag and pocket lining**
- **Tonal or contrast thread (depending on your skill level)**
- **22cm (8⅝in) of 6mm (¼in) elastic**
- **Basic sewing kit (see Materials)**

Use a 0.5cm (¼in) seam allowance, unless a different amount is stated.

CUTTING OUT

1 When cutting out the needlecord, all pattern pieces should be laid up and cut in the same direction as it has a 'pile', which means it looks a different shade one way to the opposite way. Fold the needlecord fabric in half with wrong sides together, making sure that the cord rib is running down. Pin your cut-out pattern pieces (see Patterns) onto the fabric using **Fig.1** as a guide. Cut all pieces as stated on the pattern. Mark any notches with a small snip. Transfer any other pattern markings to the fabric.

2 Cut the pocket pieces from the contrast fabric as stated on the pattern.

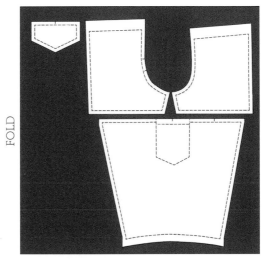

Fig.1

MAKING UP

Sewing the Upper Leg Side Seams
1 With right sides together, match one front upper leg to one back upper leg, and pin and sew at the side seam. Finish the seam using an overlocker or zigzag stitch (**Fig.2**). Repeat to join the remaining front upper leg and back upper leg.

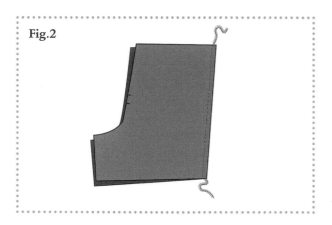

Fig.2

2 Press the seam allowances towards the back of the trousers (easily identified by the double notch on the rise). Edgestitch through all layers 3mm (¹⁄₈in) from the seam on the upper back legs (**Fig.3**).

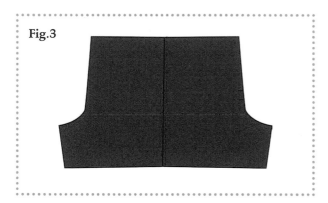

Fig.3

Making the Pocket Flaps

1 With right sides together, match one outer pocket flap with one lining pocket flap. Pin and sew around three sides, leaving the top edge open (**Fig.4**).

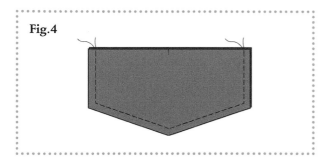

Fig.4

2 Trim the excess seam allowance from the corners. Turn through, rolling seams out to the edges. Make sure you have pushed the corners out and press flat. Trim any excess lining along the top edge, then topstitch around the pocket shape about 3mm (¹⁄₈in) from the edge (**Fig.5**).

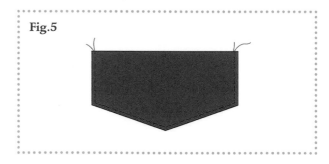

Fig.5

Sewing the Pocket Bags into the Lower Legs

1 Working on one side at a time, take a pocket bag piece and position with right sides together over a lower leg piece, making sure that the notches match and that the pocket bag extends beyond the marked stitching line. Following **Fig.6**, sew down 0.75cm (⁹⁄₃₂in) from the top edge, pivot at the corner to sew a 0.75cm (⁹⁄₃₂in) seam allowance, and pivot once more to finish at the top edge again. Snip diagonally into the corners of the seam allowance, as shown on the diagram.

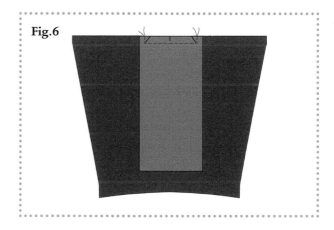

Fig.6

2 Turn the pocket bag piece to the wrong side of the lower leg and roll the seam out to create a shallow rectangular shape, and press (**Fig.7**).

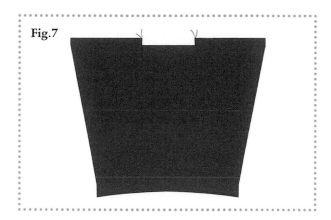

Fig.7

Attaching the Pocket Flap

1 With the lower leg right side facing up, position the pocket flap centrally over the pocket opening, matching the notches. Pin or tack (baste) in place (**Fig.10**).

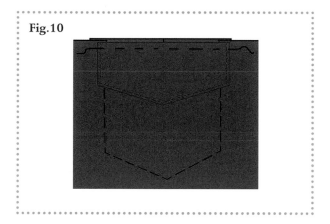

Fig.10

3 Working with the lower leg wrong side facing up, fold the unstitched edge of the pocket to the top edge of the lower leg. Press the fold and pin to hold in place (**Fig.8**).

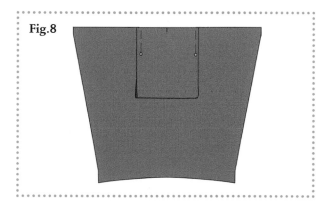

Fig.8

Attaching the Upper Legs to the Lower Legs

1 Once the pockets have been completed on each of the lower legs, it is time to attach the upper leg to the lower leg by sewing the cross seam, working on one side at a time. Take an upper leg and place it on a lower leg, right sides together, with the pocket flap sandwiched in between. (Look for the extra notch on the back leg to make sure you are positioning the correct way.) Sew the cross seam (**Fig.11**).

4 Turn the lower leg to the right side and transfer the pins to the right side so you can see them. Using the marked stitching line as a guide, sew through all layers to create the pocket bag with profile stitching (**Fig.9**). Keep the top edge open (for Ramsey to keep his maps in).

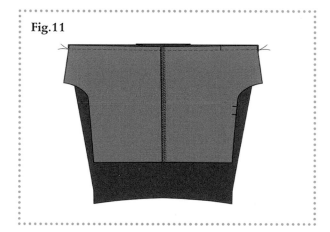

Fig.11

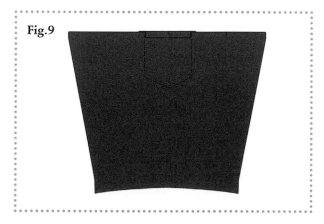

Fig.9

2 Press the seam allowance upwards and edgestitch through all layers on the upper leg (**Fig.12**).

Fig.12

3 Repeat to join the remaining upper leg and lower leg to make a mirror image.

Hemming the Legs and Sewing the Front and Back Rise

1 Finish the raw edges at the hems using an overlocker or zigzag stitch. Turn to the wrong side by 1cm (³⁄₈in) and sew in place.

2 Place the legs right sides together. Sew the front rise, then the back rise, and finish the seams using an overlocker or zigzag stitch (**Fig.13**).

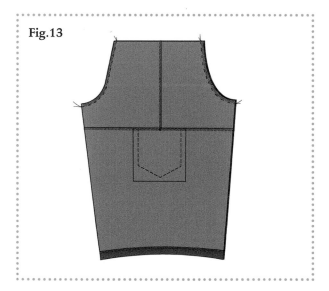

Fig.13

Sewing the Inside Legs

1 With right sides together, match and pin the inside legs (to join the front to the back), making sure the rise seams match. Sew the inside leg seams (**Fig.14**).

Fig.14

Sewing the Waist Casing

1 Finish the raw edge at the waist using an overlocker or zigzag stitch. Fold 1.5cm (⁵⁄₈in) to the wrong side and press in place.

2 Sew a line of topstitching 1cm (³⁄₈in) down from the pressed edge stopping about 1cm (³⁄₈in) short of where you started.

3 Using a safety pin attached to one end of your elastic, thread it through the opening in the waist casing, ensuring that the unthreaded end of the elastic is still accessible (**Fig.15**).

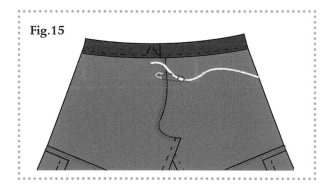

Fig.15

4 Overlap the ends of the elastic by 2cm (³⁄₄in) and join using zigzag stitch. Pull the waistband out and the joined ends of the elastic will disappear into the casing. Close the opening with machine stitching.

Ramsey's Backpack

YOU WILL NEED

- **23cm (9in) square of felt or faux leather***
- **18cm (7in) x 3cm (1¹/₈in) strip of faux leather for straps**
- **6cm (2³/₈in) of 2mm (¹/₁₆in) round leather cord for the carry handle**
- **10cm (4in) zip with plastic teeth (minimum length)**
- **Two small D rings about 1cm (³/₈in) wide**
- **Basic sewing kit (see Materials)**

Use a 0.5cm (¼in) seam allowance, unless a different amount is stated.

*Ramsey has two versions of his backpack, a faux leather one and a felt one with faux leather straps. This project is best tried in felt first then you can progress to the full 'leather' one.

CUTTING OUT

1 Cut the cut-out backpack strap pattern piece (see Patterns) from the faux leather strip. Lay the remaining cut-out pattern pieces onto a single layer of felt and cut out all pieces as stated on the pattern. Use a rotary cutter, if you have one, to cut the straps and zip edge strips into two to give nice straight edges. Mark any notches with a small snip. Transfer any other pattern markings to the fabric.

MAKING UP

Making the Zip Loop

1 With your zip right side facing up on your work surface, place the un-notched edge of one of the zip edge strips (also right side facing up) to butt up against the zip teeth. When inserting this zip, I tend not to work with a zipper foot, so make the foot choice based on your usual preferences – watch that your stitching doesn't stretch the zip edge strip. Sew close to the edge of the zip teeth, moving the pull tab out of the way as necessary (**Fig.1**) (if you are using a longer zip, you can open the zip so that the pull tab is completely out of the way).

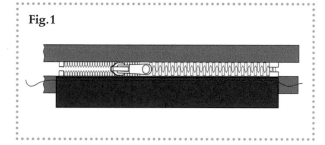

Fig.1

2 Repeat to sew the remaining zip edge strip to the other side of the zip making sure the start and end positions are level (**Fig.2**).

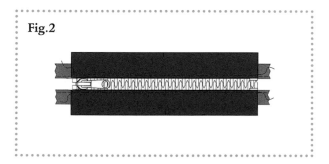

Fig.2

3 If you are working with a longer zip, to shorten, sew across the zip teeth at the lower end before trimming off the excess zip tape to be the same length as the zip edge strips. Unzip the zip. Match the upper zip tape and teeth up as though the zip is still closed and sew across the ends (**Fig.3**) to complete the zip band.

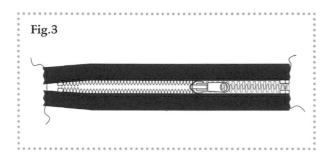

Fig.3

4 Take the underband and position it right side facing up over the bottom of the zip band so that it overlaps it by 0.5cm (¼in). Sew through all layers (**Fig.4**).

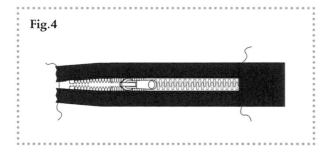

Fig.4

5 Bring the other end of the underband around to the top of the zip band and overlap it by 0.5cm (¼in) to create a loop. Sew through all layers to complete the zip loop and set aside (**Fig.5**).

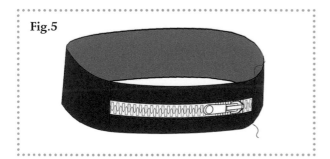

Fig.5

Sewing the Fronts

1 With right sides together, match the upper front to the lower front and sew together (**Fig.6**).

Fig.6

2 Flip up the upper front so it is right side facing, then fold up the lower front at the level of the notches on each side and finger-press in place to give the impression of a pocket. Staystitch at each side within the seam allowance (**Fig.7**).

Fig.7

Sewing the Zip Loop to the Front

1 Take your set-aside zip loop and turn it to be inside out. With right sides together, match the front panel to the zip loop using the notches at upper centre and lower centre. (The two side notches should be level with the top of the overlaps on the zip loop.) Pin in place (**Fig.8**). Before sewing, snip into the zip loop seam allowance where you can see it needs to spread to match the curves of the front panel, then stitch in place (**Fig.9**).

Fig.8

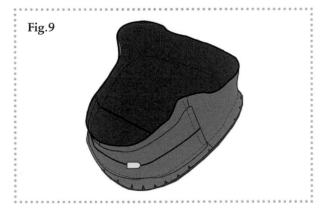

Fig.9

Positioning the Straps

1 Working on the right side of the back panel, place the long straps about 1cm (³/₈in) apart equidistant from the central notch. Taking your short length of leather cord for the carry handle, position it on top of the straps, again judging the distance so it is balanced. Staystitch in place within the seam allowance (**Fig.10**).

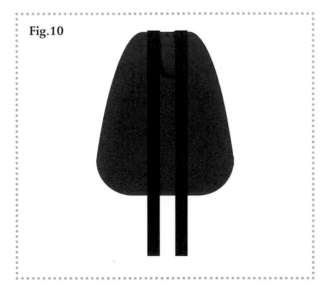

Fig.10

2 Wind the straps up so they don't get caught in the next stage.

Attaching the Back

1 Make sure the zip is fully open. Working in the same way as you did to sew the zip loop to the front panel, join the back panel to the other side of the zip loop (checking the straps are safely tucked inside) (**Fig.11**).

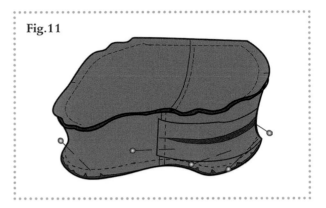

Fig.11

FINISHING OFF

1 Carefully turn the backpack right side out through the zip opening. Push and smooth the seams out.

2 Using double thread, hand sew the two D rings to the base of the backpack as marked on the underband pattern (**Fig.12**).

Fig.12

3 Thread the straps through the D rings from the outside towards the main body of the backpack and knot them to create the shoulder straps.

Luna
MEETS THE
Mayor

When Granny was younger there had been a food shortage during a terrible war and she had volunteered to be a land girl. Granny was very proud of the work she had done as a land girl and it was here that she had met Daisy the Herdwick. Every day working hard and laughing harder. After the war, the two had remained great friends their whole lives, seeing each other as much as they could and reminiscing about the days they had spent together and the trouble they had got into, from the secret parties they had thrown in the hay barns to the long rambles on the fells.

Daisy had dreamed of becoming the first female mayor of the small grey town she lived in, she wanted to preserve what made the town special. Before Luna's granny had left, she gifted Daisy a crook and the most beautiful dress that she had ever owned. All Daisy's clothes had been plain greens and browns to help her blend into her beloved landscape, but this dress was a twirling red and white gingham delight, which reminded Daisy of all the picnics they had eaten together on warm summer days. Daisy treasured it; she had worn that dress for every milestone event in her life. When it had become worn out, Granny had replaced it. Daisy was instantly recognisable by her gingham dress.

Daisy had grown up to fulfil her dreams of becoming mayor; ever headstrong and determined she was now in her ninth term with no intention of giving up her role. Things hadn't always been easy but it was a dream well-lived. Daisy arrived home after a meeting to find the unfamiliar car in her driveway but no sign of her guests. Perhaps Luna had gone for a walk, she thought, and put on the kettle.

As more time passed Daisy began to worry and asked her neighbours to see if anyone had seen a pretty grey rabbit. They told her that they had seen a rabbit, a badger and a squirrel some hours ago. All the shops in town would be closed by now and the weather was dreadful, this was indeed cause for concern. How would Daisy ever explain to her old friend that she had lost her granddaughter! Daisy grabbed her woolly coat and crook and pinned a note to the door: "Luna, I've come to find you", then set out in the rain to find the rabbity hare.

Daisy knocked on door after door but no one could tell her anything. Eventually the houses became more and more infrequent and Daisy grew wetter and wetter. As Ramsey's house came into the distance, she knew she was going to have to ask him for help. Ramsey was such a pain, Daisy thought. He was always arguing with her about planning permissions and new shops in town, he never let anything be easy. She understood his views and knew that in many ways she agreed with him but when you are mayor you have to listen to what everyone wants.

Daisy should have just stayed inside and waited but doing nothing wasn't in her nature. She really hoped the grumpy old ram would drive her home and would have even accepted the gloating it would come with to be safe against the storm. As Daisy approached the house she could hear laughter, the light seeped from the window in a glow that felt far more comforting than Daisy thought anything about Ramsey could be. She knocked on the door expecting to see a scowling sheep but was instead greeted by a familiar young rabbit.

"Thank goodness you're safe Luna!" and then her eyes met the ram's. "You!" they said in unison and began to argue about everything and anything.

"Stop it!" shouted Freddie, Rowan and Luna, and the two sheep looked at them in surprise.

They explained that Ramsey had rescued them from the fellside and had intended to take them back to town but couldn't get his car to start, there was no working telephone because Ramsey lived off grid and there was no choice other than to wait out the rain. Luna was so sorry they hadn't been able to get in touch. The weather outside worsened and it became clear that no one was going anywhere. Daisy and Ramsey sat scowling at each other from across the room, and one by one they fell asleep in front of the fire.

Luna was the first to wake the next morning. Ramsey was snoring in the chair opposite. Luna tiptoed to the bathroom to splash her face and saw Daisy asleep in Ramsey's bed. Luna was surprised by this act of kindness considering the animosity between them.

When the rain stopped Ramsey set about trying to fix his car. Luckily for everyone Daisy knew a thing or two about biofuel engines. Luna noticed that although they still seemed to squabble, there was a softer tone and Luna even caught them smile at each other once or twice. Maybe they had more in common than they thought…

Daisy's Twirling Dress

YOU WILL NEED

- **40cm (16in) x 150cm (60in) gingham fabric**
- **40cm (16in) x 150cm (60in) dress net**
- **1.3m (1½yd) of 5cm (2in) wide broderie anglaise trim**
- **Two 1cm (³/₈in) heart-shaped buttons**
- **Two 6mm (¼in) press studs**
- **2.5cm (1in) iron-on transfer for pocket decoration (optional)**
- **Basic sewing kit (see Materials)**

Use a 0.5cm (¼in) seam allowance, unless a different amount is stated.

CUTTING OUT

1 With wrong side facing upwards, fold the edges of the gingham fabric in to meet in the middle to give you two folded edges. Now you will be laying out your pattern pieces onto the right side of the fabric. Pin your cut-out pattern pieces (see Patterns) onto the fabric using **Fig.1** as a guide and keep a large remnant for cutting out the pocket later. Cut all pieces as stated on the pattern. Mark any notches with a small snip, including an 'on the fold' snip to mark the top centre point of the front and back skirt pieces. Transfer any other pattern markings to the fabric.

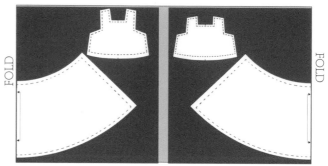

Fig.1

2 Fold your dress net fabric in the same way so that the edges meet in the middle. Pin your two skirt pattern pieces on the folds and cut out. Remember to mark the top centre point of the front and back skirt pieces with 'on the fold' snips.

MAKING UP

Sewing the Outer and Lining Front Bodices Together

1 With right sides together, match the outer front bodice to the front lining and pin around the armholes and neckline. Sew, pivoting to turn corners (see Machine Sewing Techniques: Turning a Corner). Trim the excess seam allowance from the corners and snip into the inner corners (**Fig.2**).

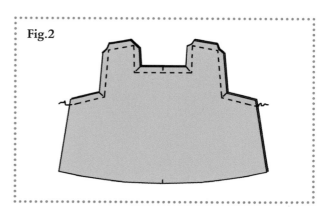

Fig.2

2 Turn the pieces to be right side out, then use a knitting needle or similar to push out the corners of the shoulder straps. Roll the seams out to the edges and press flat (see Techniques: Pressing) (**Fig.3**).

Fig.3

Sewing the Outer and Lining Back Bodices Together

1 The outer back bodice is attached to the back lining in exactly the same way as before, but you'll notice that the back neckline is higher than on the front bodice and the straps extend further (**Fig.4**).

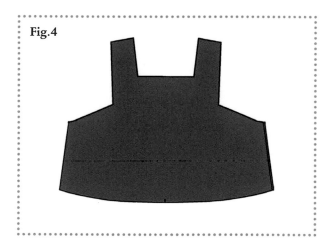

Fig.4

Sewing the Bodice Side Seams

1 Pull the front and back bodices upwards, so that you can see the wrong side of the linings and also the armhole seams. Working one side at a time, match and pin one front armhole seam to one back armhole seam. Then match and pin the rest of the seam, front to back. Sew along the seam. Repeat with the other side (**Fig.5**).

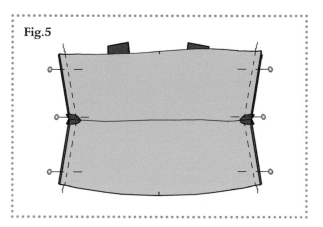

Fig.5

2 Press the side seams open, then pin and tack (baste) the bottom edges of the bodice outer to the lining (**Fig.6**).

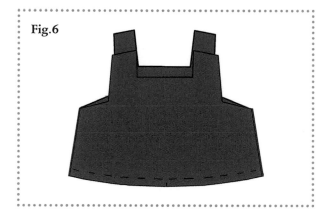

Fig.6

Sewing the Skirt Side Seams

Note: the skirt side seams are sewn together with a French seam, which encloses the raw edges for a neat finish.

1 With right sides facing out, match the front and back outer (main fabric) skirt pieces and pin the side seams together. Sew using a just less than a 0.5cm (¼in) seam allowance (**Fig.7**) and press the seam allowance to one side.

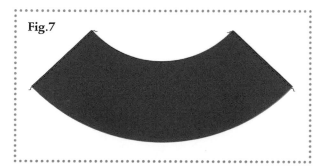

Fig.7

2 Turn the skirt so that the wrong sides are facing out, and press the seams flat along each edge. Sew each side seam again, this time using a 0.75cm (⁹/₃₂in) seam allowance. This encloses the previous seam to create a French seam (**Fig.8**).

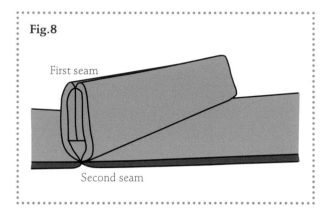

Fig.8

First seam

Second seam

3 Repeat steps 1 and 2 to sew the front and back net skirt pieces together but give your iron a chance to cool first as the net can melt very easily.

Joining and Gathering the Skirts

1 With the outer skirt turned to the wrong side, put the right side of the net skirt to the wrong side of the outer skirt (seams on both skirts will be facing upwards, to wrong side). Match notches and pin, then tack (baste) in place around the waist circle.

2 Sew lines of gathering stitches around the waist of the joined skirt, stopping and starting at the side seams (**Fig.9**) (see Machine Sewing Techniques: Gathering).

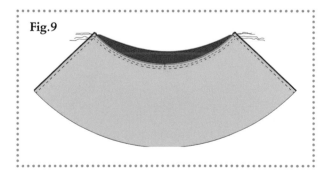

Fig.9

3 Gather up the top threads, first from one end then the other, until the waistline of the skirt roughly measures the same as that of the bodice. Ensure that the ends of the gathered threads remain visible and usable.

Sewing the Skirt to the Bodice

1 With the skirt wrong (net) side facing out, slide the bodice inside the waist of the skirt so that right sides are together, matching the side seams of the bodice to the skirt, then pin. Now adjust the gathering tension so that the notches on the centre front and centre back of the skirt match those on the bodice. Make sure your gathers are even and double check that the side seams match.

2 Sew all the way around the waist through all layers using a 1cm (³/₈in) seam allowance – I tend to do this with the gathering facing upwards (net side uppermost), so I can keep my eye on the fullness of the fabric around the waist (**Fig.10**).

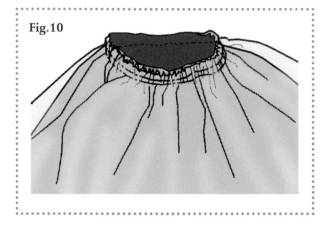

Fig.10

3 Turn through to the right side and remove any visible threads from the gathering stage, including any tacking (basting) stitches. Turn back to the wrong side and finish the waist seam allowance using an overlocker or zigzag stitch. Press the seam towards the bodice.

Attaching the Broderie Anglaise Trim

1 If your broderie anglaise trim has an undecorated wavy raw edge, cut it off to give you a straight edge to work with. Press 1cm (³/₈in) of the end of the trim to the wrong side.

2 With right sides together, line up the folded edge of the trim to one of the skirt side seams. Keeping the net under-skirt out of the way, sew the trim to the hem of the outer skirt only (**Fig.11**). Be aware that the hem is cut on the bias and will stretch more than the trim, so pin and tack (baste) as necessary to control this step. Just before completing the hem circle, measure the trim to be 1cm (³/₈in) past the side seam and sew to this cut edge (**Fig.12**). Press the seam allowance up towards the skirt of the dress and slip stitch the ends of the trim to one another along the fold (see Hand Sewing Techniques: Slip Stitch). Give the dress a final press.

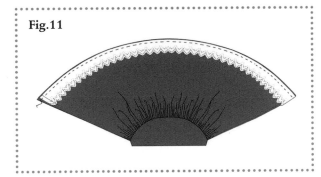
Fig.11

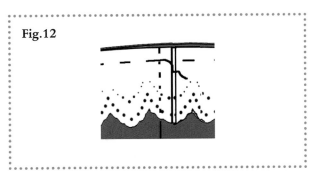
Fig.12

Making and Decorating the Pocket

1 Pin two layers of the remnants of your main fabric right sides together (roughly 8.5cm/3¼in square). Use the heart pocket template to draw a heart shape onto one side of your fabric sandwich. Place a pin within the heart shape to hold the layers in place as you sew.

2 Starting at A, sew along your marked line to B, slowly working around the curves (**Fig.13**).

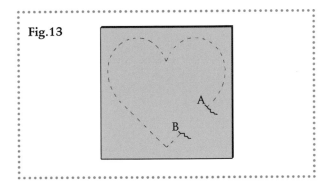
Fig.13

3 Trim the heart shape down to about 0.5cm (¼in) away from your stitching line. Snip into the inner corner and trim away the excess curve and corner fabric. Fold and press back the seam allowance at the opening (**Fig.14**). Turn the heart shape through to the right side, pushing out the points and rolling the seam to make sure the curves are nice and smooth. Slip stitch the opening closed.

Fig.14

4 If using the optional iron-on transfer, apply it now. Place it in position rough side down onto the front of the heart and press using a high heat and a pressing cloth. Leave to cool for a few minutes (do not press again otherwise you will end up with a sticky mess).

FINISHING OFF

1 Place the pocket in position on the left-hand side of the skirt of the dress (as worn) and sew in place, leaving an opening at the top for Daisy to put useful things in. You can try using machine edgestitch, but because of the gathering you may find it is easier to slip stitch it on by hand.

2 Sew the press studs into position as marked, sewing one half of each press stud onto the front of the dress and the other half onto the underside of the back shoulder strap (**Fig.15**). Then sew the decorative heart buttons onto the topside of the back shoulder straps (**Fig.16**).

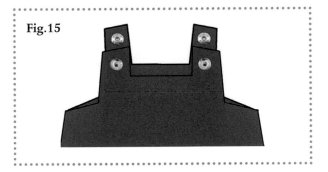
Fig.15

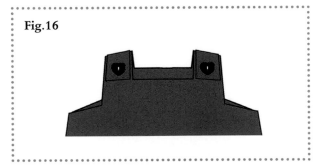
Fig.16

Luna AND THE SALTY Seadog

Hugh Houndslow came from a long line of hounds; he was maybe the houndiest hound you could ever meet. His long ears drooped either side of his face and he had an awfully good bark. Hugh was a fine chap who liked to boast of his pedigree, something that Granny had mostly ignored. Luckily for Luna, Hugh had been the headmaster at Ralph's school and the two still kept in touch. Luna knew that Granny and Hugh had not spoken in a few years and had devised a cunning plan. She had persuaded Ralph that they should launch her new collection of nautical-inspired dresses on an actual boat, and Hugh was quite the seadog. Eager to show his mastery of the sea off to anyone Hugh hastily agreed.

Ralph and Luna arrived mid-afternoon, the deck of the boat caught the sun in a way that took Luna by surprise, how very grand it seemed! The hound seemed so much younger than Granny, his coat ruffled by the wind and his cravat perfectly positioned at his neck.

Hugh greeted Ralph with a warmth that softened his face; he recognised Luna immediately, pulling her into a wide blanketing hug.

"You must be Luna Lapin! You look just like your granny. The fun we used to have. Your granny was quite the mischief maker, would you believe it," he chuckled. "I miss your granny, very much, never have I had a better friend."

"Then why aren't you talking to each other?" Luna didn't understand why the two of them had stopped speaking when it was so obvious they loved each other very much.

Hugh sighed, "If I'm going to tell this story we best all sit down."

Once Luna and Ralph were comfortably nestled in the cabin Hugh began his tale.

"Luna, I'm not sure what you know about your granny when she was young, but let me tell you, she was whip-smart and even more stubborn than she is now. We immediately hit it off and spent all our downtime together. There was a big group of us and your granny was the heart and soul of every activity, dance or debate. There was me, a fine old fox called Francis, who moved to America, Minerva and Minnie the Pine Marten twins," (Luna had already written to the Martens and they had said of course they would come to the party), "Misha the Russian Bear, who joined us as an exchange student, your dear grandfather" (Luna had never met her grandfather, but knew he must have been very wonderful indeed), "and, of course, Ottoline Ottonburgh." Hugh looked wistful as he said her name, he had been in love with Ottoline Ottonburgh for what felt like his whole life.

Everyone knew Ottoline Ottonburgh, the great naturalist who explored the world and wrote marvellous books all about her adventures. Luna knew she and Granny had been friends but had no idea they were such good friends!

"Anyway, as our days at university drew to a close we planned one final perfect summer together. Ottoline was going to teach us all to sail and we would journey up to her family home in the Scottish Western Isles. Oh, what a summer we should have had but, as plans do, things shifted and changed, Francis's family moved to America and he decided to leave with them, the twins got offered jobs together and knew an opportunity like that would not arrive again. And Misha fell madly deeply in love with a young deer called Rosie who got frightfully seasick and he couldn't bear to be apart from her. So that left just your granny and grandad, Ottoline and myself, and I couldn't face it, with your granny and grandad so in love whilst I didn't have the courage to tell Ottoline how very much I loved her."

"Your granny begged me to come. She said all I needed to do was to be brave and tell Ottoline how I felt but I couldn't stand the idea that she might not love me back, so the scared dog I was, I hid the truth and abandoned my friends. They couldn't go without me, there wouldn't be enough to man the deck, so the trip was cancelled and our friendship seemed to come to an end. Only later did I find out that your grandad had planned a magnificent proposal to your granny on that trip surrounded by their dearest friends and I had let them all down with my cowardice. Ottoline sailed off on her first exploration instead, your granny and grandad married, and I dedicated myself to work to avoid thinking about all I had lost."

Luna felt sorry for the hound now, surrounded by all his things but quite alone. "Granny misses you too," she said. "She talks about you all the time and is always asking Ralph how you are. You really should come to her party, she would love to see you... it seems so silly not to after all these years!"

Hugh thought about it and made a decision he should have made long ago, and every time he felt his eyes dampen when he saw a picture in the newspaper of the brave otter he loved so much.

"Thank you, Luna but first I really must find Ottoline and tell her how I feel. You know I learnt to sail so that one day I could find her and do exactly as your granny asked of me!"

"How romantic" Ralph purred.

Hugh's Matelot Top

YOU WILL NEED

- 20cm (8in) x 60cm (24in) striped jersey
- Basic sewing kit (see Materials)

Use a 0.5cm (¼in) seam allowance, unless a different amount is stated.

CUTTING OUT

1 Fold the fabric in half so that right sides are together. Pin your cut-out pattern pieces (see Patterns) onto the fabric using **Fig.1** as a guide. Positioning the hems of the front/back pieces on the same stripe will help with matching stripes on side seams. Cut all pieces as stated on the pattern. Mark any notches with a small snip.

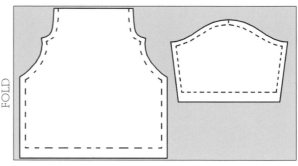

Fig.1

MAKING UP

Sewing the Neck and Shoulder Seams

1 With right sides together, match and pin the neck and shoulder seams on the front and back pieces. Using a stretch stitch or a small zigzag (length 2.5, width 2), sew down the neck edge and across the shoulder on each side (**Fig.2**).

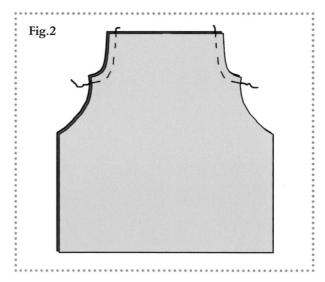

Fig.2

Sewing and Attaching the Sleeves

1 With right sides together, match and pin a sleeve onto each armhole and sew together (**Fig.3**). Turn 1cm (³/₈in) to the wrong side and zigzag the sleeve hems in place, taking care not to stretch the fabric as you sew.

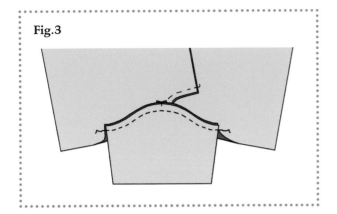

Fig.3

Sewing the Underarms and Side Seams

1 With right sides together, pin the underarm and side seams together, taking care to match stripes (if using striped fabric), and sew (**Fig.4**).

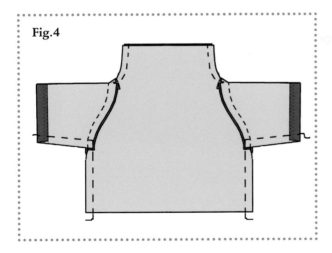

Fig.4

FINISHING OFF

1 Turn 1cm (³/₈in) to the wrong side at the hem and zigzag in place, taking care not to stretch the fabric as you sew (**Fig.5**).

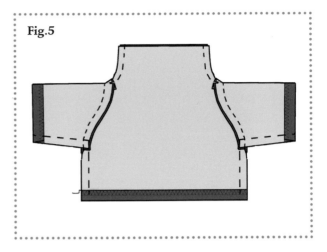

Fig.5

2 Fold 1.5cm (⁵/₈in) of the neckline to the wrong side and hand sew in place with a couple of tacking (basting) stitches at each shoulder seam to hold in position (**Fig.6**). Trim all ends and turn through to the right side.

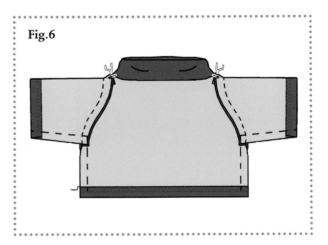

Fig.6

Hugh's Button-Front Trousers

YOU WILL NEED

- **One fat quarter of quilting weight or mid-weight linen mix fabric**
- **Six 6mm (¼in) doll buttons**
- **Four press studs**
- **12cm (5in) of 0.5cm (¼in) wide elastic**
- **Basic sewing kit (see Materials)**

Use a 0.5cm (¼in) seam allowance, unless a different amount is stated.

CUTTING OUT

1 With wrong side facing upwards, fold the edges of the fat quarter in to meet in the middle to give you two folded edges. Now you will be laying out your pattern pieces onto the right side of the fabric. Pin your cut-out pattern pieces (see Patterns) onto the fabric using **Fig.1** as a guide. Cut all pieces as stated on the pattern. Mark any notches with a small snip. Transfer any other pattern markings to the fabric.

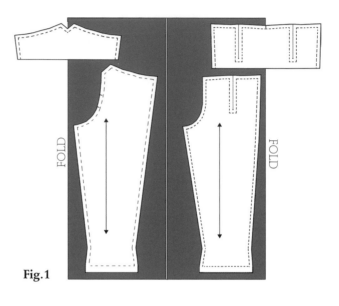

Fig.1

MAKING UP

Sewing the Front Rise and the Front Facing

1 Place the front pieces right sides together and sew the front rise (**Fig.2**). Press the seam allowance open at the waist.

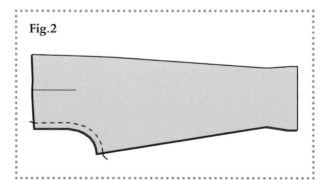

Fig.2

2 Finish the lower edge of the front facing using an overlocker or zigzag stitch.

3 With right sides together, match and pin the front facing to the front trousers around the waist, and sew as marked by the dashed line in **Fig.3**, pivoting at the corners. (You can cut a paper guide to mark your sewing lines if you wish – see Patterns: Hugh's Button-Front Trousers Stitching and Button Guideline.)

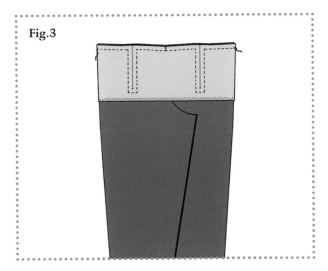

Fig.3

4 Snip the seam allowances into the corners (**Fig.4**) and trim off excess seam allowance at corners. Turn right side out, taking time to create nice sharp corners, and press the shape flat. Topstitch 0.5cm (¼in) away from the inner edges as shown in **Fig.5**.

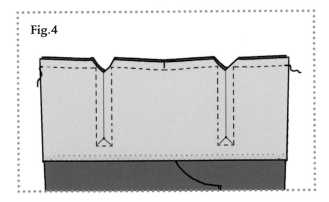

Fig.4

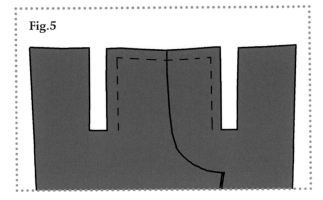

Fig.5

5 Take each topstitched edge, overlap the opposite edge by the depth of the topstitching to form a pleat and pin the pleats in place, then sew a line of topstitching between the two edges to secure (**Figs. 6 and 7**).

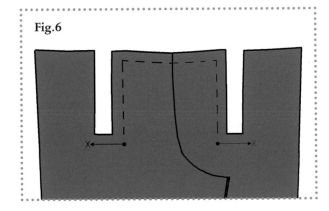

Fig.6

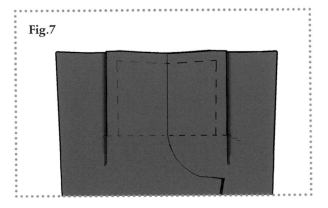

Fig.7

Sewing the Back Rise and the Back Facing

1 With right sides together, sew the back rise leaving a gap (for Hugh's tail) between the two notches (**Fig.8**). Press the seam allowance open at the waist.

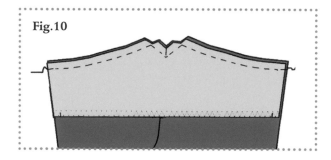

Fig.10

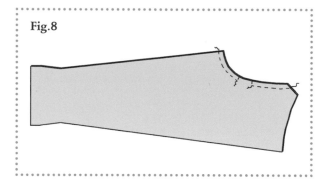

Fig.8

2 Finish the lower edge of the back facing using an overlocker or zigzag stitch. With right sides together, match and pin the back facing to the back trousers around the waist, matching the V in the facing to the centre back seam. Sew along the top edge, pivoting at the corners (**Fig.9**). Trim the seam allowances at the corners and snip into the centre of the V (**Fig.10**). Turn right side out and press the shape flat.

Sewing the Side Seams

1 Fold the back facing side seams in by 0.5cm (¼in) and press in place. Moving the back facing out of the way, match the front (including front facing) and back legs at the side seams and sew (**Fig.11**). Finish the side seams using an overlocker or zigzag stitch and press towards the back.

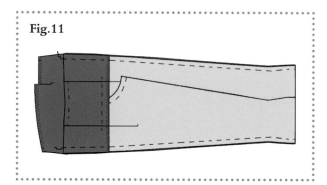

Fig.11

Fig.9

Making the Back Casing

1 The back of the trousers is elasticated. To make a casing for the elastic, readjust the back facing to sit flat and matching at the side seams, and pin. Sew a line of stitching across the back facing through all layers 1cm (³/₈in) up from the bottom edge, then another 1cm (³/₈in) up from this (**Fig.12**).

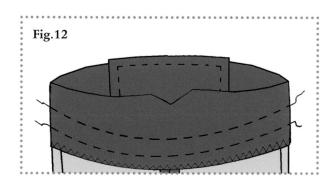

Fig.12

2 Using a safety pin attached to one end of your elastic, thread it through the channel. With 1cm (³/₈in) protruding on one side, sew it in place, then pull out 2cm (¾in) on the other side and sew down along side seam. Trim off excess elastic.

Hemming and Sewing the Inside Legs

1 To hem the trouser legs, turn 0.5cm (¼in) to the wrong side and then a further 0.5cm (¼in). Press and then edgestitch through all layers (**Fig.13**).

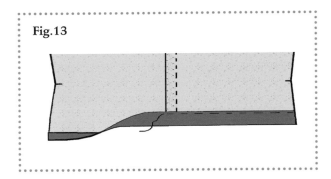

Fig.13

2 With right sides together, match and pin the inside legs – front to back – making sure the rise seams match, then sew (**Fig.14**). Turn trousers through to the right side.

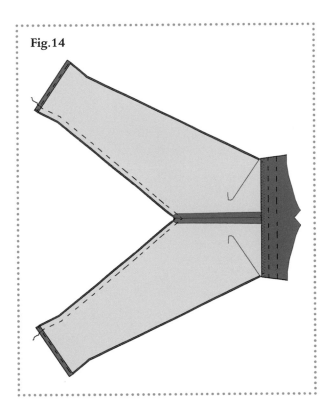

Fig.14

FINISHING OFF

1 Sew three buttons on each side of the centre front flap as marked on the paper guide (see Patterns: Hugh's Button-Front Trousers Stitching and Button Guideline).

2 Position one side of a press stud under each of the top two buttons on each side and sew in place. Then sew other half of each press stud onto the front facing to correspond with the button positioning of the top two buttons, referring to your paper guide. Trim all ends.

3 If you prefer, you could fold back the hemmed edges of the legs when worn by Hugh for a deep turnup.

Hugh's Peacoat

YOU WILL NEED

- 23cm (9in) x 90cm (36in) felt for main fabric
- 25cm (10in) x 65cm (26in) 100% cotton fabric for the lining (includes quantity for the bandana)
- Iron-on anchor motif or similar
- Eight 9mm (³/₈in) metal buttons
- Basic sewing kit (see Materials)

Use a 0.5cm (¼in) seam allowance, unless a different amount is stated.

CUTTING OUT

1 Fold the felt fabric in half with wrong sides together. Pin your cut-out pattern pieces (see Patterns) onto the fabric using **Fig.1** as a guide. Cut all pieces as stated on the pattern. Mark any triangles with a small snip to the centre and mark any notches with a small snip. Transfer any other pattern markings to the fabric.

FOLD

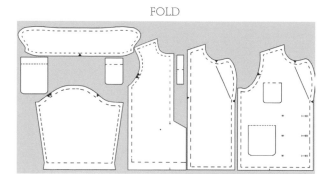

Fig.1

2 With wrong side facing upwards, fold in the short ends of the lining fabric to meet in the middle to give you two folded edges. Now you will be laying out your pattern pieces onto the right side of the fabric. Pin your cut-out pattern pieces (see Patterns) onto the fabric using **Fig.2** as a guide and cut out, again transferring any other pattern markings. (Set aside the bandana piece ready to make that project later.)

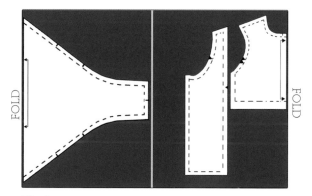

Fig.2

MAKING UP

Making and Attaching the Pockets

1 Fold 1cm (³/₈in) on the top edge of each of the patch pockets and on the breast pocket to the wrong side and press. Fuse the anchor motif onto the smallest (breast) pocket (**Fig.3**).

Fig.3

2 Position the pockets onto the front panels using the pattern as a guide, and machine stitch in place using a small zigzag (width 2, length 2) with the right needle drop falling off the edge of the pocket. The left-hand side as worn has a breast pocket and a lower patch pocket, while the right-hand side has a lower patch pocket only (**Fig.4**).

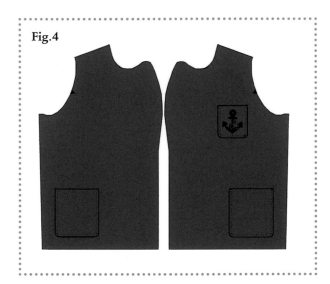

Fig.4

Sewing the Centre Back Seam and Back Vent

1 With back panels right sides together, sew the centre back seam, stopping at the first dot (to allow for the vent) (**Fig.5**). Press seam to left-hand side as worn. Fold back the vent facing on the left-hand side (as worn) from the end of the line of stitching to the snip in the hem and press in place.

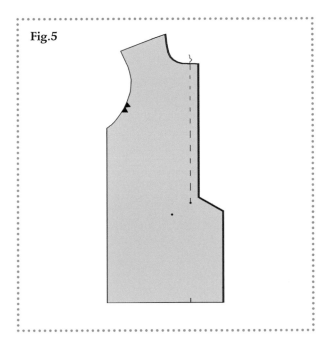

Fig.5

2 With the wrong side facing up, trim 1cm (³/₈in) off the vent width on the right-hand side (as worn) (**Fig.6**).

Fig.6

3 Pin the right-hand vent so it sits over the left-hand vent at the hem. Turn the joined panels so that the right side is facing up, then edgestitch the centre back seam down the left-hand side as worn. When you reach the level of the vent, pivot to head at an angle to stitch to the second dot (marked vent topstitch point on the pattern) (**Fig.7**).

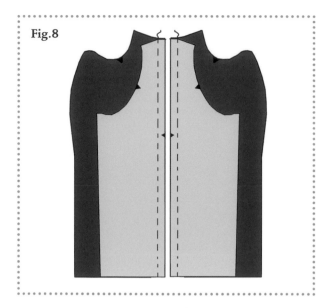

Fig.8

Fig.7

Sewing the Shoulder Seams

1 With right sides together, match the shoulder seam of one front to one back shoulder seam and sew together. Repeat with the other front and the remaining back shoulder seam (**Fig.9**). Press seams open.

Fig.9

Sewing the Front Facing to the Front Lining

1 With right sides together, sew one front facing to one front side lining, matching notches. Repeat with other front facing and front side lining (**Fig.8**). Press seams open.

Attaching the Back Buggy Lining

1 Hem the back buggy lining by turning 0.5cm (¼in) to the wrong side and then a further 1cm (³⁄₈in). Press and then edgestitch through all layers (**Fig.10**). At the neckline, pinch the two notches together to form a small pleat and tack (baste) to one side (**Fig.11**).

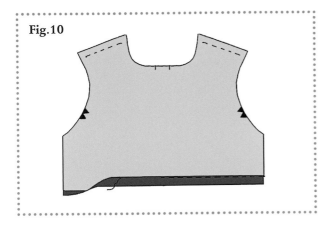

Fig.10

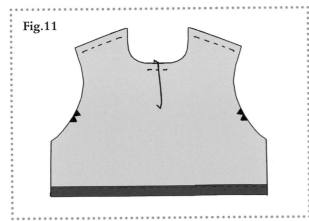

Fig.11

2 With right sides together, match the shoulder seam of one front facing/lining to one back buggy lining shoulder seam and sew. Repeat with the other front facing/lining and the remaining back buggy lining shoulder seam (**Fig.12**). Press seams open and set aside.

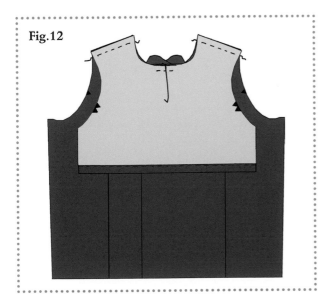

Fig.12

Making the Epaulettes

1 Fold one of the epaulette pieces in half so that the short edges match and edgestitch around three sides leaving the edge opposite the folded one unstitched. (If your machine tends to eat small projects, just fold without stitching.)

2 Position the epaulette so that it is central to the shoulder seam and the unstitched edge slightly overhangs the armhole. Tack (baste) in place at the armhole. With double thread, hand sew a button near the folded end through all layers. Repeat to attach the remaining epaulette piece to the other shoulder seam (**Fig.13**).

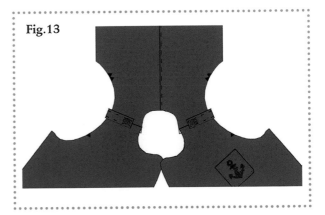

Fig.13

Making the Collar

1 With right sides together, match and pin the two collar pieces. Sew around the outer edge (**Fig.14**) (use the machine's hand wheel to control the tight curves if you need to).

Fig.16

Fig.14

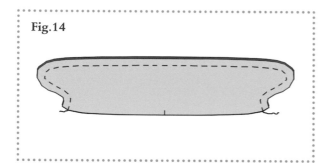

2 Trim the seam to 2mm (¹⁄₁₆in) and trim off the corners to reduce the bulk. Turn through to the right side. Press flat, ensuring the seam is right on the edge, and edgestitch (**Fig.15**).

2 Now take the jacket lining and place it on top, right sides together, taking care to match the notches around the neck edge, the curve of the front edge, the side seams, etc. Pin in place all the way around the jacket front hems, front edges and neckline, then sew together (**Fig.17**).

Fig.15

Fig.17

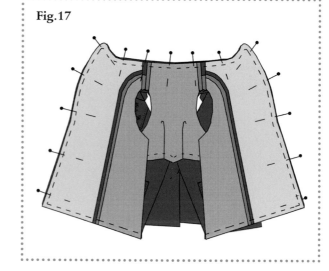

Preparing the Front Edge and Attaching the Collar

1 With the outer jacket right side facing up, position the collar so the open edges line up with the notches on the jacket fronts. Match it to the neckline using the centre back seam as a guideline. Pin in place and tack (baste) if you choose to (**Fig.16**).

3 Turn through to the right side to check the collar is caught in the seam all the way along. If all is okay, trim the corners and trim the neck seam allowance to 0.25cm (³⁄₃₂in) to reduce the bulk.

4 Turn through to the right side once again and push the corners out. Roll seams out to the edges and press flat.

Sewing the Sleeves

1 Hem the sleeves by turning 1cm (⅜in) to the wrong side. Press and then edgestitch through all layers.

2 With right sides together, match one sleeve to the armhole using the notches to position. Pin in place and sew together. Repeat with the other sleeve. Press seam allowance towards the sleeve (**Fig.18**).

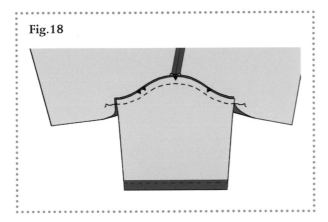

Fig.18

Sewing the Side Seams

1 Smooth the back buggy lining down so that it matches the back body at the underarm and pin at the side seam.

2 With right sides together, and keeping the front lining out of the way, match up the sleeve seams, underarm and side seams of the main jacket and pin, then sew in place. Note that the coat back is longer than the front, so stop sewing at the level of the hem on the front leaving you with approx. 1cm (⅜in) extra length on the back. Press seams to the front (**Fig.19**).

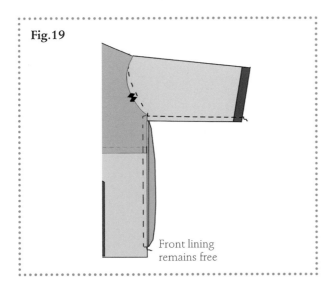

Fig.19

Front lining remains free

3 Turn the seam allowance on the front lining side seam to the wrong side and then match and pin the folded edge up to the stitching line of the side seam ready for the next stage.

This photograph shows one of Hugh's many peacoats with a different lining to his bandana – if you are following our instructions, the lining will match the bandana.

Sewing the Back Hems

1 Press the back hems up by 1cm (⅜in), opening up the back vent facing to press up the hem and then fold it back down. Slip stitch the hems in place by hand (see Hand Sewing Techniques: Slip Stitch) and continue up the side seams to hold the front lining in place (**Fig.20**).

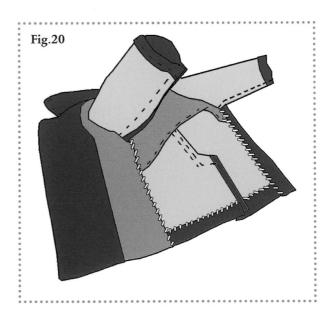

Fig.20

FINISHING OFF

1 To finish the back vent, start at the existing stitching and sew parallel to the fold down to the hem (**Fig.21**).

Fig.21

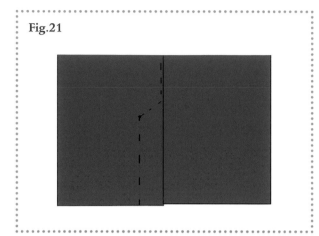

2 Using double thread, hand sew buttons on the left- and right-hand sides of the jacket front following the positions marked on the front pattern. Make three small buttonholes on the right-hand side as worn, practising first on some scrap felt if necessary (see Machine Sewing Techniques: Making Buttonholes).

3 Using a warm iron, press the lapels down so that the break point (where the lapels start to fold back) is level with the first buttonhole.

Hugh's Bandana

YOU WILL NEED

- **100% cotton fabric (quantity is included in Hugh's Peacoat)**
- **Basic sewing kit (see Materials)**

Use a 0.5cm (¼in) seam allowance, unless a different amount is stated.

CUTTING OUT

1 Pin your cut-out pattern piece onto the fabric using the layout for Hugh's Peacoat lining as a guide and cut out as stated on the pattern. Mark any notches with a small snip into the fabric.

MAKING UP

Sewing the Seams
1 Unfold the cut-out bandana piece and fold it in half the other way, right sides together, making sure that the points and notches match. Sew around the unfolded edges, leaving a turning gap between the two notches on one side (**Fig.1**).

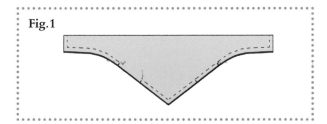

Fig.1

2 Trim the excess seam allowance at the corners and turn through to the right side. Push the points out using a knitting needle or similar. Roll the seams to the edges and press flat. Slip stitch the opening closed (**Fig.2**) (see Hand Sewing Techniques: Slip Stitch).

Fig.2

FINISHING OFF

1 To wear, tie a knot at the back of Hugh's neck.

Luna
AND THE
unexpected guest

On the morning of Granny's party a letter arrived for Luna with a photograph of Hugh Houndslow and Ottoline Ottonburgh smiling arm in arm on a small boat somewhere chilly looking. Luna flipped the photo over to read:

Dearest Luna,
We hope that you will visit us as our love story is far too long to tell in a simple letter. Please bring Granny if she can make the trip. Please tell her how very sorry we are that we spent so long avoiding love when she told us so many times to be braver, just as she has always been.
Warm wishes,
Hugh and Ottoline.

Granny thought that this would be the best gift she would receive all day but she was very wrong. Granny had no idea what was in store for her. Alfie was to keep Granny busy all afternoon, and if anyone knew how to waste time it was Alfie. Luna, with the help of all her friends, decorated Granny's garden: it was dripping in bunting, roses and peonies adorned every vase on every table. The buffet of deliciously-prepared greens and sweet treats smelled heavenly. Soon guests would be arriving. Luna couldn't wait to see Granny's face light up with surprise.

Daisy was the first to arrive wearing her red gingham dress, she had left her crook behind and instead held Ramsey's hand in its place. Ramsey looked a little less scruffy and adjusted his vegan leather backpack nervously. Rowan began to tease the sheep mercilessly and despite their old age they blushed like teenagers on a first date.

As more and more people arrived the party buzzed with anticipation for Granny's arrival. They all stood very still, hiding from view. The front door clicked and Luna heard Granny tell Alfie that she was going to get a drink. Luna groaned, "Come on Alfie, hurry her up!"

Luna heard the front door open again.

"I am so sorry I am late to the party!" said a honey-thick voice in an accent Luna didn't recognise. Luna groaned again, the surprise was ruined!

"Hellooooo!" said the voice in the almost empty house, "I thought there was a birthday party, I have an invitation."

Luna wondered who it might be, the voice definitely had a European lilt to it. Misha and Rosie had said they were too old to make such a journey and would send their own surprise.

Luna wondered if this voice could be it!

The rest of the guests all looked to Luna not knowing what to do. Luna could see Alfie through the window, shrugging his shoulders. Luna was so upset her surprise had been ruined by this unexpected guest and had no idea what to do!

"Hello! Is anyone here?" said the voice again.

Granny answered: "You must have the wrong house, my dear, there's no party here, but it is my birthday, so why don't we share some cake."

"Let's go in the garden Granny," said Alfie with undeniable urgency. By this time the guests had started to chatter quietly.

The back door opened and there stood a glorious doe, dressed in glossy velvet with the biggest eyes you could imagine. Everyone shouted "Happy Birthday" and the doe looked guiltily backwards at Granny who was still in the kitchen.

"I'm so sorry, my name is Freya and I didn't mean to ruin your party," she said. Luna looked at her in a very un-Luna like manner.

"Oh my!" said Granny, "I would never have guessed you had planned a party for me Luna," and the old rabbit winked! Luna began to laugh and took Freya's hand.

"You didn't ruin it!" said Luna. "Nothing gets past Granny. You must be Misha and Rosie's surprise."

Granny chuckled. Apparently Alfie had let it slip months ago, even before the visit to Daisy! Granny had got the whole truth out of him in seconds. "There's nothing that young one won't do for one of his granny's shortbreads," Granny said with her mischievous grin and Alfie just shrugged.

Freya explained she was on tour with the Russian Opera and had come on her parents' request to perform at the party. What a glorious gift! As Freya began to sing, Luna looked at Granny with her friends and saw her for the first time as not just her granny, but as a wonderful rabbit that had touched the lives of so many. Granny looked younger than she had in years and Luna hoped she could be as many things to as many creatures as Granny was.

Luna's friends stood together talking about how lucky they were to have a friend as quiet and kind and thoughtful and honestly good as Luna Lapin. It was because of this impeccably dressed rabbit each one of them was so much better than they had been before they met her. Luna walked towards them and they pulled her into a great big hug.

"What was that for?" she giggled.

"Because we love you, Luna," they said.

Freya's Halterneck Playsuit

YOU WILL NEED

- **50cm (20in) x 75cm (30in) shot taffeta fabric (includes lining for Freya's Opera Coat)**
- **150cm (59in) of 2.5cm (1in) wide fusible hemming tape**
- **One 6mm (¼in) press stud**
- **Basic sewing kit (see Materials)**

Use a 0.5cm (¼in) seam allowance, unless a different amount is stated.

CUTTING OUT

1 Although shot taffeta does not really have a right or a wrong side, it does have a direction or nap, so do follow the layout guide provided. Fold the fabric in half and pin your cut-out pattern pieces onto the fabric using **Fig.1** as a guide (note that the layout includes the lining for Freya's Opera Coat). Cut all pieces as stated on the pattern. Mark any notches with a small snip and transfer any other pattern markings.

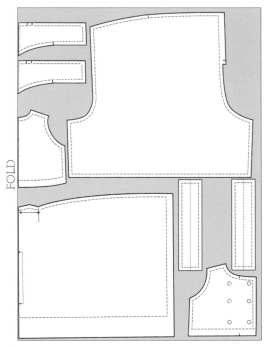

Fig.1

MAKING UP

Making the Halterneck Straps

1 With right sides together, fold each strap piece in half so that the long edges match. Sew 0.5cm (¼in) from the unfolded edge and along one short edge. Trim at the corners and turn each strap through using a turning tool. Press flat and set aside (**Fig.2**). (In reality the straps will now look a little curvy rather than straight but that's okay.)

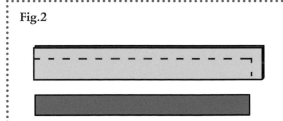

Fig.2

Sewing the Straps into the Bodice Front

1 Take one bodice piece, right side facing up, and position the straps so that they sit between the notches aligning the raw edges of the straps with the straight edge of the bodice (**Fig.3**). Pin in place.

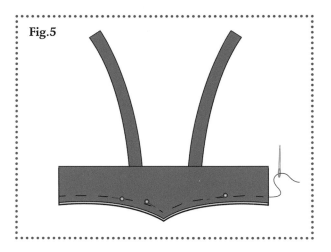

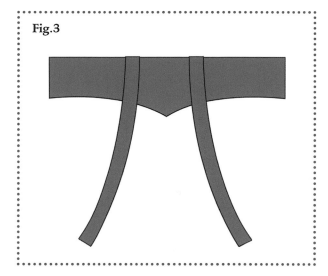

2 Now place a second bodice piece, right side facing down, on top, sandwiching the straps in between. Sew up one side, along the top edge and down the other side (**Fig.4**).

Preparing the Lower Legs for the Bloomers

1 With wrong sides together, press each leg cuff in half with long edges together (**Fig.6**).

2 Sew lines of gathering stitch 0.25cm ($^3/_{32}$in) and 0.75cm ($^9/_{32}$in) from the cuff edge of each bloomers piece (**Fig.7**) (see Machine Sewing Techniques: Gathering).

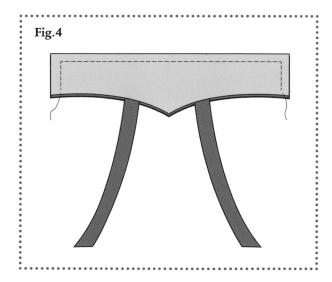

3 Cut off the excess seam allowance at the corners and turn through using a turning tool inner to push out the corners. Pin, then tack (baste) the layers together at the lower edge (**Fig.5**).

3 Gather up the top threads, first from one end then the other, to roughly measure 13cm (5in) (**Fig.8**). Ensure that the ends of the gathered threads remain visible and usable.

Fig.8

4 With right sides together, match and pin the gathered bottom of each leg to the raw edge of a folded cuff. Adjust your gathers to be even and sew together, working with the gathers upwards so you can see what is going on. Finish the seam allowance using an overlocker or zigzag stitch. Press the seam upwards (it will want to head downwards!) (**Fig.9**).

Fig.9

5 Working one leg at a time and with right sides together, match and pin the inside leg seams and sew. To do this you need to smooth the area near the seam flat, pushing the gathering away (**Fig.10**).

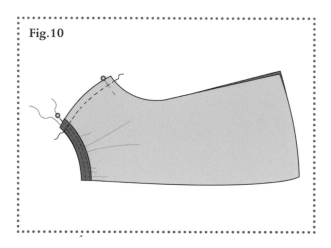

Fig.10

Sewing the Crotch

1 Turn one leg right side out and slide it, cuff first, inside the other leg (**Fig.11**).

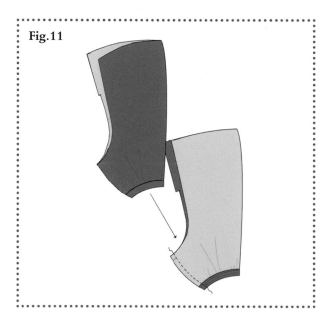

Fig.11

2 Matching the inside leg seams, pin and sew the crotch, finishing at the level of the notch on the back rise (**Fig.12**). Turn the bloomers through to the right side (**Fig.13**).

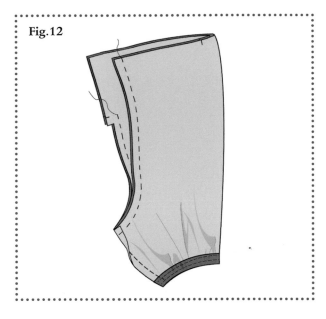

Fig.12

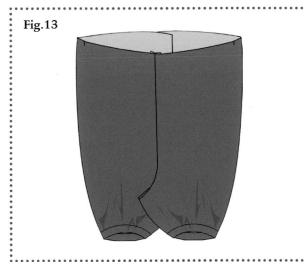

Fig.13

Preparing the Skirt

1 With right sides together, fold the skirt in half and sew down 2cm (¾in) to the dot to make the front pleat (**Fig.14**).

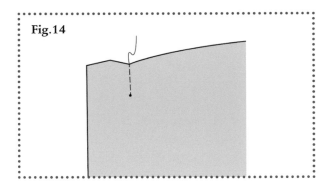

Fig.14

2 Press the pleat flat and open on the wrong side and staystitch in place at the top edge (**Fig.15**).

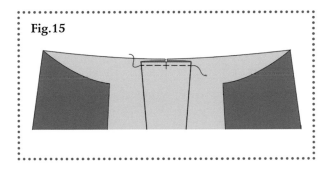

Fig.15

3 Finish the side seams using an overlocker or zigzag stitch, then press the hem up by 3cm (1⅛in) and use fusible hemming tape to fix in place.

Joining the Bloomers to the Skirt

1 With the right sides facing out, match the skirt to the bloomers around the top edge and pin or tack (baste) in place. Sew lines of gathering stitch 0.25cm (³⁄₃₂in) and 0.75cm (⁹⁄₃₂in) from the top edge (see Machine Sewing Techniques: Gathering), starting to sew 1cm (³⁄₈in) in from the edge at the notches.

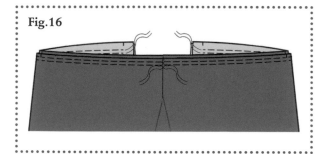

Fig.16

2 Break your stitching at the pleat line at the centre front, then start again on the other side, finishing stitching 1cm (³/₈in) in from the edge (**Fig.16**).

3 Gather up the top threads from the back to the centre front, first from one end then the other, to roughly match half the width of the bodice. Repeat to gather the top threads on the other half of the joined skirt/bloomers. Ensure that the ends of the gathered threads remain visible and usable.

Attaching the Bodice

1 Working on one side at a time and with right sides together, match the gathered edge of the joined skirt/bloomers to the bodice, matching the centre front notch on the skirt to the centre of the upside-down V on the bodice. The sides of the bodice should match up to the notches at the start and finish of the gathering stitches (**Fig.17**).

Fig.17

2 Fold the joined skirt/bloomers seam allowances over at one side of the bodice to sandwich it in between, and sew from the edge to the centre front using a 0.5cm (¼in) seam allowance (see **Fig.18**, left-hand side).

3 Repeat steps 1 and 2 to sew the other half of the bodice to the joined skirt/bloomers (**Fig.18**, right-hand side).

Fig.18

4 Pull the bodice upwards to turn the corners out. Remove any visible threads from the gathering stage and finish the seam allowance using an overlocker or zigzag stitch. Press the seam allowance downwards.

Sewing the Centre Back Seam

1 With right sides together, sew the seam at the centre back of the skirt using a 1cm (³/₈in) seam allowance, stitching from the hem to the notch (**Fig.19)**

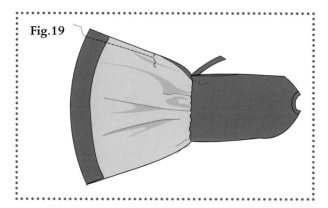

Fig.19

FINISHING OFF

1 Sew one half of a press stud under the left-hand side of the back of the bodice and the other half on the upper right-hand side, about 1cm (³/₈in) from the edge at each side.

2 When Freya is wearing the playsuit, tie the halterneck straps at the back of her neck.

Freya's Opera Coat

CUTTING OUT

1 All pattern pieces should be laid up and cut in the same direction and our layouts follow these principles. Run your hand down the fabric to establish the direction (it will feel smoother one way). With wrong side facing upwards, fold in the selvedges of the velvet fabric as shown to give you two folded edges. Now you will be laying out your pattern pieces onto the right side of the fabric. Pin your cut-out pattern pieces (see Patterns) onto the fabric using **Fig.1** as a guide. Cut all pieces as stated on the pattern. (Note that the taffeta lining pieces were cut in Freya's Halterneck Playsuit instructions.) Mark any notches with a small snip, including an 'on the fold' snip to mark the centre back points on the skirt and back pieces. Transfer any other pattern markings.

Fig.1

YOU WILL NEED

- **20cm (8in) x 150cm (60in) velvet for main fabric**
- **Shot taffeta for lining fabric (quantity is included in Freya's Halterneck Playsuit)**
- **Six 6mm (¼in) buttons**
- **Four plastic press studs (optional)**
- **Fusible hemming tape (quantity is included in Freya's Halterneck Playsuit)**
- **Basic sewing kit (see Materials)**

Use a 0.5cm (¼in) seam allowance, unless a different amount is stated.

MAKING UP

Preparing the Back Skirt

1 Finish the side seams of the back skirt using an overlocker or zigzag stitch. With right sides together, fold the back skirt in half and sew down to the dot to make the back pleat (**Fig.2**).

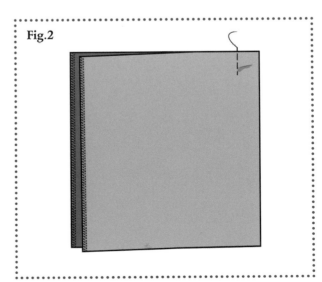

Fig.2

2 Bring the centre back notch to the seam you just made, smoothing the extra layers flat, and staystitch in place at the top edge (**Fig.3**).

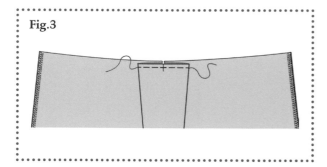

Fig.3

3 Sew lines of gathering stitch along the top edge (see Machine Sewing Techniques: Gathering). Gather up the top threads, first from one end then the other, to roughly measure 15cm (6in), checking it against the width of the back piece that it will be sewn to (**Fig.4**). Ensure that the ends of the gathered threads remain visible and usable. Set aside.

Fig.4

Preparing the Front Skirt
1 Finish the side seams of each of the front skirt pieces using an overlocker or zigzag stitch. Sew lines of gathering stitch along the top edge, finishing at the notch closest to the front edge (**Fig.5**).

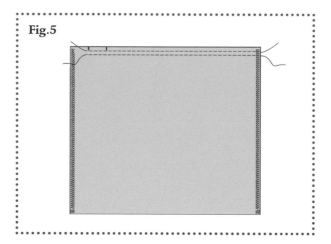

Fig.5

2 Pull up the gathering stitches so that each front skirt piece measures roughly 9cm (3½in) on the top edge. Ensure that the ends of the gathered threads remain visible and usable. Set aside.

Sewing the Shoulder Seams
1 With right sides together, match and pin one back shoulder seam to one front shoulder seam and sew together. Repeat to sew the remaining front to the back at the shoulder seam (**Fig.6**). Press seams to the back

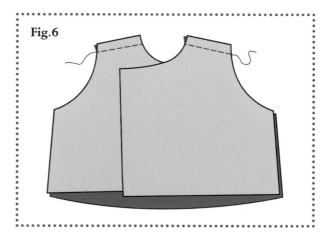

Fig.6

2 Repeat step 1 to join the front lining pieces to the back lining piece, but this time press to the front.

Joining the Lining to the Top

1 With right sides together, match the edges of the lining to the outer pieces around the neckline and the front edges. Pin, then tack (baste) in place. Starting at the lower edge of one front and pivoting at the corners, sew along the edge, carefully following the curve of the neck, to finish at the lower edge of the other front (**Fig.7**).

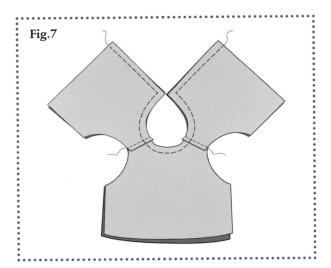

Fig.7

2 Trim excess seam allowances to 0.25cm (³/₃₂in) around the curve of the neck and trim the corners. Snip into the seam allowance through the neck curve to sit flat once turned.

3 Turn the top of the coat right side out, using a knitting needle or similar to push out the corners. Roll seams out to the edges and press the edges of the front and the neck flat. Work to match the outer and lining at the lower edges, side seams and armholes and tack (baste) in place (**Fig.8**).

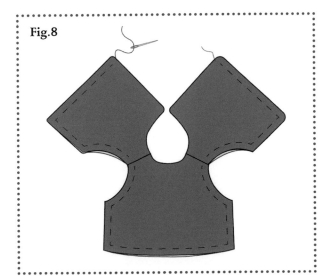

Fig.8

Sewing the Sleeves

1 Finish the raw edge of each sleeve hem using an overlocker or zigzag stitch. Hem the sleeves by turning 1cm (³/₈in) to the wrong side and press. Sew in place about 0.75cm (⁹/₃₂in) from the edge (**Fig.9**).

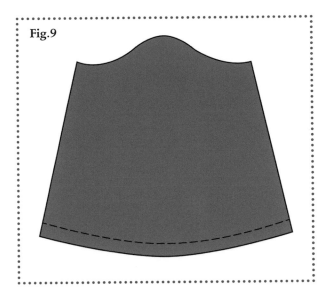

Fig.9

2 With right sides together, match one sleeve to the armhole using the top notch to match the shoulder seam. Pin in place and sew together. Repeat to sew the other sleeve in place. Press seam allowances towards the sleeves and finish using an overlocker or zigzag stitch (**Fig.10**).

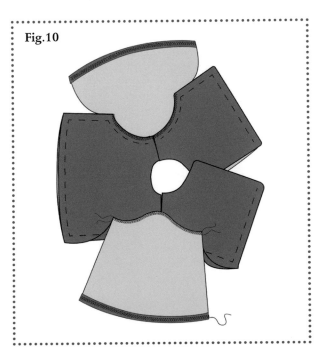

Fig.10

Attaching the Back Skirt to the Upper Back

1 With right sides together, match the gathered edge of the back skirt to the bottom edge of the upper back, matching the centre back notches. Adjust your gathers to be even and sew together using a 1cm (³/₈in) seam allowance (**Fig.11** shows the view from the back skirt and **Fig.12** shows the view from the upper back). I normally like to sew with my gathers upwards so I can better see what's going on, but this is a bit bulky so you may find that it is better to tack (baste) in place and turn to the flatter side to sew. Finish the seam allowance with an overlocker or zigzag stitch and remove any visible threads from the gathering stage. Press the seam downwards.

Attaching Front Skirts to Upper Fronts

1 With right sides together, match and pin the gathered edges of the front skirts to the bottom edge of the upper fronts, matching the centre front notches. The upper fronts align with the second notch where the gathering stitches finish on the skirts (**Fig.13**).

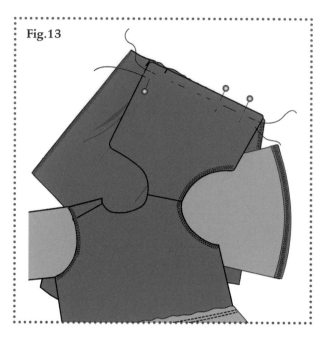

Fig.13

2 Before sewing one side at a time, tightly wrap the extended edge of the front skirt backwards over the upper front edge to sandwich it in between. This will create a front skirt facing in step 3. Sew the waist seam using a 1cm (³/₈in) seam allowance (**Fig.14**).

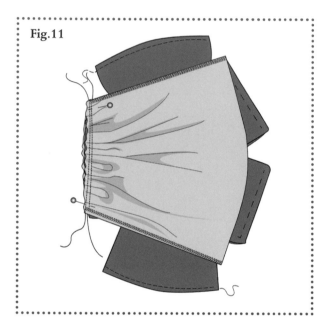

Fig.11

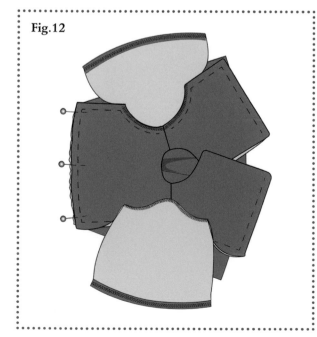

Fig.12

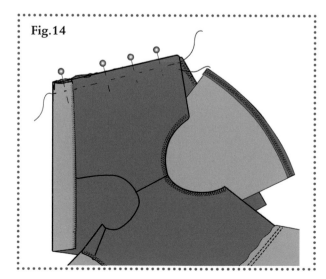

Fig.14

3 Finish the waist seam allowance using an overlocker or zigzag stitch. Turn the front facing to the inside and press the edge. Remove any visible threads from the gathering stage and press the waist seam downwards.

Sewing the Side Seams

1 With right sides together, match and pin the underarm seam on the sleeves and the side seams on the top and skirt of the coat and pin together. Sew, pivoting at the underarm and at the waist. Finish the seam allowance using an overlocker or zigzag stitch (**Fig.15**).

Fig.15

Hemming the Coat

1 The intended hem is 3cm (1¹⁄₈in) deep. Fold the front skirt facings back on themselves – so right sides are together. Sew across this turning at the depth of the hem (**Fig.16**). Trim off the corner excess and cut the facing seam allowance back.

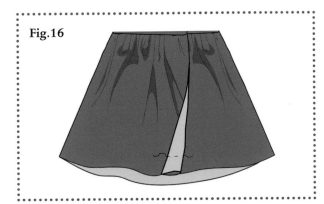

Fig.16

2 Press the rest of the hem up by 3cm (1¹⁄₈in) and hand sew in place with herringbone stitch, or use hemming tape to fuse it in place (**Fig.17**).

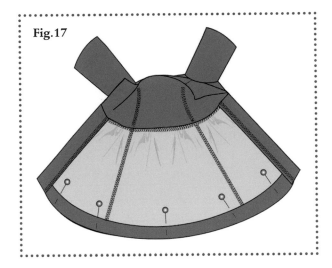

Fig.17

FINISHING OFF

1 Press studs are optional depending on whether Freya's coat will be worn closed. Sew the buttons in place on the upper front of the coat as marked on your pattern piece on the right-hand side as worn. At positions A, B and C, sew one half of a press stud on the reverse side of the coat front, right-hand side (as worn). Then sew the other half of each press stud on the front side of the coat front, left-hand side (as worn) at positions A, B and D (**Fig.18**).

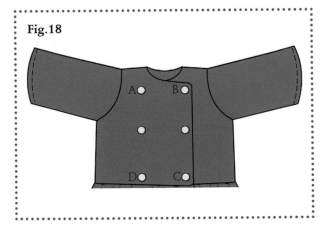

Fig.18

Freya's Music Satchel

YOU WILL NEED

- 14cm (5½in) x 25cm (10in) felt fabric
- Six-stranded embroidery cotton (floss) in tonal colour
- Two 1cm (³/₈in) wide buckles (inner width)
- Two press studs
- Two 1cm (³/₈in) wide D rings
- Basic sewing kit (see Materials)

Use a 0.5cm (¼in) seam allowance, unless a different amount is stated.

CUTTING OUT

1 Pin your cut-out pattern pieces (see Patterns) onto the felt using **Fig.1** as a guide. Cut all pieces as stated on the pattern. Mark any notches with a small snip and transfer any other pattern markings.

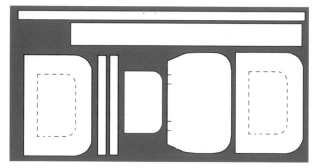

Fig.1

MAKING UP

Attaching the Pocket to the Front

1 Position the pocket onto the front body piece and sew around the sides and curved bottom edge using embroidery thread and a decorative blanket stitch (see Techniques), leaving the top edge open. Make your stitches about 3mm (¹/₈in) deep and the same distance from each other (**Fig.2**).

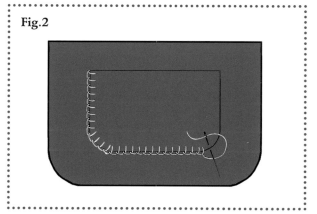

Fig.2

Preparing the Flap and Sewing on the Straps

1 Sew around the edge of the flap with blanket stitch but don't sew the straight (back) edge yet. Take the two flap straps and position them onto the satchel flap following the marked guidelines. Sew in place using a decorative running stitch, and continue on to the free end of the strap to come back up and secure the other side (**Fig.3**).

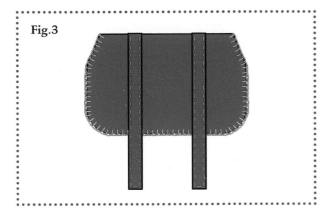

Fig.3

Inserting the Gusset

1 Match and sew one edge of the gusset to the front panel, using a decorative blanket stitch and curving the gusset to run smoothly around the corners. Repeat to sew the other edge of the gusset to the back panel. If you find your gusset is slightly long you can trim it back to be level with the main bag (**Fig.4**).

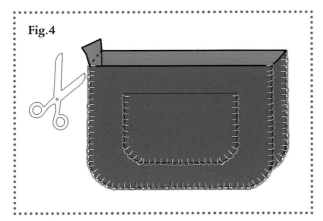

Fig.4

Attaching the Flap

1 Position the flap onto the back panel, overlapping it by 1cm (³/₈in), and sew the flap in place using a decorative blanket stitch. Make a small hole in the centre of each strap roughly 0.5cm (¼in) from where it joins the main flap. Working on one strap at a time, take a buckle and with the end with the prong nearest to it, thread the strap under the end bar and push the prong upwards through the hole, then thread the end of the strap under the opposite end bar (**Fig.5**).

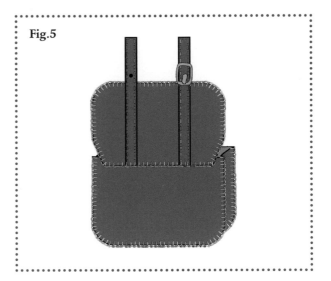

Fig.5

FINISHING OFF

1 Use a decorative blanket stitch to finish the long edges of the body strap. With double thread, hand sew a D ring to each side of the satchel, 1.5cm (⁵/₈in) down from the top of the gusset. At each D ring, thread the body strap through from the outside towards the main body of the satchel and bringing the end up by about 1cm (³/₈in), hand sew it to the inside of the strap to secure the loop (**Fig.6**).

Fig.6

2 Use your pattern piece to find the press stud positions. Sew one half of each press stud behind the straps on the flap and the other half on the main body of the bag.

HOW TO
sew Luna
AND friends

In this section we cover how to sew the animal bodies. Most of the process involves hand sewing, although there are parts that can be completed on a machine and these are noted where appropriate. You will find that Luna, Rowan and Freya follow the same body construction, although their heads and tails differ. Hugh, Daisy and Ramsey share a different body construction, but again there are variations that are individual to each one. Where animals have common elements, you'll find shared pattern pieces clearly identified in the first part of the patterns section, which has blue-bordered pages to help you find them easily. The animals are roughly 40.6cm (16in) tall when finished, but can wear any of the outfits in this book or that have been designed for Luna or her other friends.

How to Make Luna

YOU WILL NEED

- **23cm (9in) x 92cm (36¼in) light grey felt**
- **15cm (6in) x 20cm (8in) cotton lawn fabric**
- **12.5cm (5in) x 12.5cm (5in) mid-weight fusible interfacing**
- **Two 10mm (³⁄₈in) buttons for eyes and two 15mm (⁵⁄₈in) buttons for arm joints**
- **Wool yarn for tail (optional)**
- **Toy stuffing about 120gm (4½oz)**
- **Six-stranded embroidery cotton (floss) in brown for facial features**
- **Basic sewing kit (see Materials)**

Use a 0.5cm (¼in) seam allowance, unless a different amount is stated.

CUTTING OUT

1 Pin the cut-out pattern pieces (see Patterns) onto the partially folded felt, using the layout in **Fig.1** as a guide. Cut the pieces out and mark any triangles or notches with a tiny snip in the felt. Transfer all other pattern markings using tailor's tacks or a water-soluble pen.

2 Cut out a pair of ears and a pair of footpads from the lawn fabric. Cut out a pair of ears from interfacing. Mark the notches as before. Transfer all other pattern markings using tailor's tacks or a water-soluble pen.

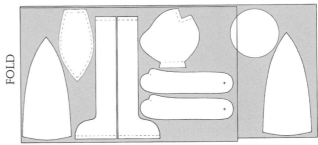

Fig.1

MAKING UP

Making the Ears

1 Using an iron, fuse the interfacing to the wrong side of the cotton lawn ears. Place the right side of a cotton lawn ear onto one felt ear, matching edges and sew around the edges, leaving the bottom open (**Fig.2**). You can machine sew or use a backstitch (see Hand Sewing Stitches: Backstitch). Repeat to make the second ear.

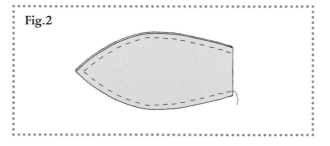

Fig.2

2 Trim the seam allowance off at the points and then turn each ear through to the right side. Use a knitting needle or similar tool to carefully push the shape out. Roll the seams out to the edge between your fingers and press flat with a warm iron.

3 Sew through the ear layers to hold them together on a central line, trying to keep your stitches invisible on the felt side. Finish about two-thirds of the way up. Fold each ear in half lengthways, enclosing the lawn fabric (**Fig.3**), and pin in place.

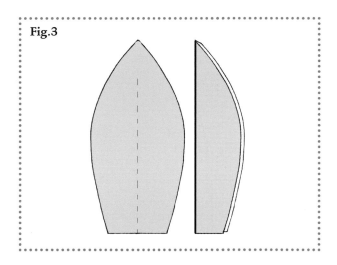

Fig.3

Making the Head

1 Line up the bottom of an ear with the straight edge of a head piece, making sure the open (cotton lawn fabric) edges of the ear are facing the nose. Fold the head piece over to cover the ear as in **Fig.4**. Make sure that the ear is tucked right up to the fold point. Sew through all layers on the marked sewing line. Use a backstitch or sewing machine for this stage. Repeat this step with the other ear and the other head piece, but make sure it is all the opposite way to the first one.

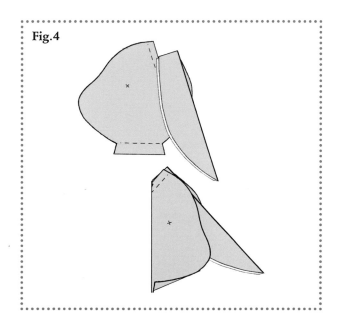

Fig.4

2 Turn the head pieces out to the right side and pin the centre front seams together so that the edges are level and the ear seams match up. Oversew the two pieces together, leaving the neck opening free (**Fig.5**).

Fig.5

3 Stuff the head through the neck opening using small pieces of stuffing to build up the shape (**Fig.6**). Tuck the neck seam allowance up into the head.

Fig.6

Making the Legs

1 Oversew two leg pieces together down the long back seam. Starting from the foot, sew the front seam up to just over the foot (**Fig.7**).

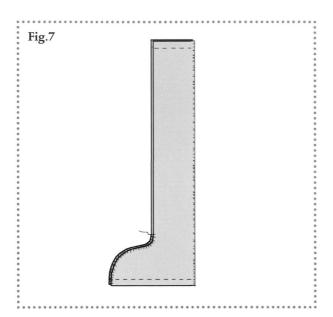

Fig.7

2 Now turn the leg so that these seams are to the inside and pin the footpad in place, using the notches on the footpad to match up with the seams you have just sewn. Ease the footpad in place and sew all the way around using a backstitch (**Fig.8**). Turn the foot back to be right side out with the raw edges enclosed and stuff the foot firmly. Resume oversewing the front leg seam, stuffing the leg firmly as you go. When you have completed one leg, repeat for the other leg. Leave about 1cm (³⁄₈in) at the top with no stuffing. The legs should be the firmest stuffed part of the bunny (and the same length). At the top, fold each leg so that the front and back seams are in line with one another to close the opening and either pin or sew together.

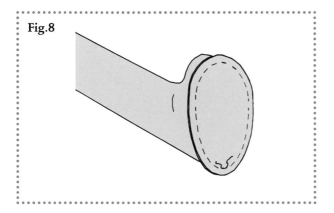

Fig.8

Making the Body

1 Take two of the body pieces and oversew down one edge. Sew the third body piece onto another free side, and then join the remaining two free edges together, starting at the lower edge of the body and finishing after about 5cm (2in) before fastening off (**Fig.9**). Turn inside out, so that the seams are to the inside ready for the next stage.

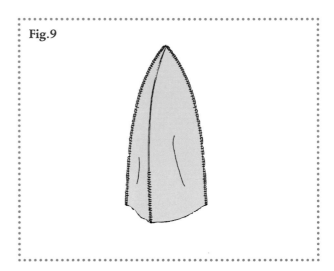

Fig.9

2 Push the legs inside the turned body. Feed them in through the opening in the body seam left in the previous step. Position the flattened top of each leg level with one of the lower edges of the body so that the outside edge of each flattened leg is in line with a tummy seam and the toes are facing up towards the tummy. Sew in place using a backstitch or tacking (basting) stitch (**Fig.10**).

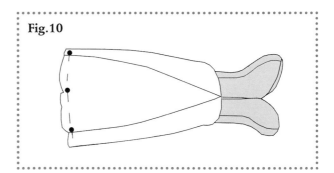

Fig.10

3 Take the circular base and matching up the three notches to the three seams of the body, enclose the raw edges of the legs and using a backstitch sew through all layers of the tummy, legs and base using a 0.75cm (⁹⁄₃₂in) seam allowance (**Fig.11**). A double thread is better when sewing through four thicknesses of felt. Complete the sewing around the circle.

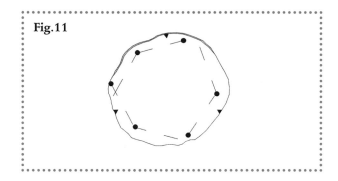

Fig.11

2 Stuff the arm firmly and then close the opening. Repeat this process to make a second arm.

3 Stitch the arms onto the body so that the top of the arm matches the level of the neck seam. Check you have the thumbs facing forwards. Position the buttons on the arms using the pattern piece as a guide. Use a double thread and a large needle to sew the arms onto the body, going through the whole body and passing through the buttons on each side (**Fig.14**). Don't pull the arms in so tight that they change the shape of the body, but just enough to pull the arms in snug to the body. Secure by passing the needle through at least fifteen times – this needs to be secure as you will be moving the arms frequently to dress Luna.

4 Turn the body back out so that the legs are dangling. Stuff the body and sew down the opening, starting from the top and meeting up with where you had previously sewn. Make sure that you use enough stuffing for the body to be firm.

5 Check you have enough stuffing in the head, but still a gap for the point of the body cone. Push the point of the body cone into the head and pin in place (**Fig.12**). Using a medium-size darner needle and double thread, sew the head to the body using a slip stitch and ensuring it is well attached by going around the neck at least twice.

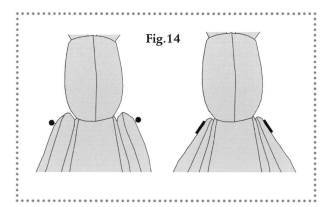

Fig.14

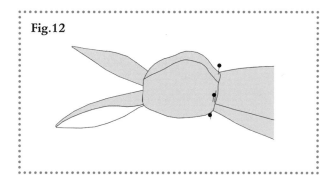

Fig.12

FINISHING OFF

1 Using three strands of brown embroidery thread, sew on buttons for eyes in a similar way to the arms, checking the pattern piece for positioning. Add both eyes at the same time, sewing through the face, but this time pulling the eyes in slightly to indent the face a little.

2 Use three strands of embroidery thread to satin stitch a triangular nose (see Hand Sewing Stitches: Satin Stitch). The top of the nose should measure 6.5cm (2½in) from the ear/head seam. The nose should be about 1cm (⅜in) wide at its widest point.

3 Adding a tail is optional. Using the wool, make a pompom for the tail by winding the wool around a credit card or piece of stiff card. Snip down both edges and bind the centre with a remnant of wool. Shape and fluff up the wool and then trim with a pair of scissors to be about 2cm (¾in) in diameter. Sew the tail onto the back seam of the body just above the base. Luna is now ready to be loved and dressed.

Making the Arms

1 Match two arm pieces and sew together starting at the back of the arm. Oversew over the arm top, down the front and down to the hand (**Fig.13**). Use a deeper stitch to define the thumb and then oversew until you are 4cm (1½in) away from where you started.

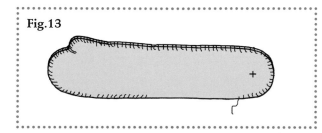

Fig.13

How to Make Hugh

YOU WILL NEED

- **25cm (10in) x 90cm (36in) main felt (brown)**
- **23cm (9in) x 23cm (9in) contrast felt (snow white)**
- **5cm (2½in) x 5cm (2½in) black felt**
- **Two 10mm (³⁄₈in) buttons for eyes and two 15mm (⁵⁄₈in) buttons for arm joints and tail**
- **Toy stuffing about 120gm (4½oz)**
- **Two 20mm (¾in) self-cover buttons**
- **1m (39in) of 0.8mm elastic thread**
- **Basic sewing kit (see Materials)**

Use a 0.5cm (¼in) seam allowance, unless a different amount is stated.

CUTTING OUT

1 Pin the cut-out pattern pieces (see Patterns) onto the main (brown) felt (partially folded), using the layout in **Fig.1** as a guide and noting which pieces should be cut in which colour. Pin the relevant pieces onto single layer contrast (white) felt leaving as much spare for the optional freehand body patches. Cut the pieces out and mark any triangles or notches with a tiny snip in the felt. Transfer all other pattern markings using tailor's tacks or a water-soluble pen.

2 Cut a nose out of black felt as well as a 4cm (1½in) x 1cm (³⁄₈in) strip (also for the nose).

Fig.1

MAKING UP

Making the Ears
1 Match up two ear pieces and fold in half keeping the corners together (don't let the inside ear slip outwards). Backstitch (or machine sew) in a diagonal line from the corner of the ear to the point of the dart, marked with a dot on the pattern (**Fig.2**). Repeat with the remaining two ear pieces to make the second ear.

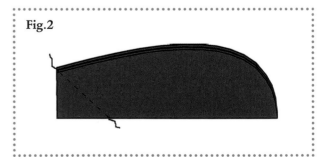

Fig.2

Making the Head

1 With right sides together, match and pin the upper head to the under flews (or jowls). Backstitch (or machine sew) around the long curved edge (**Fig.3**). Turn the seam allowance to the inside and roll the seam to the edge.

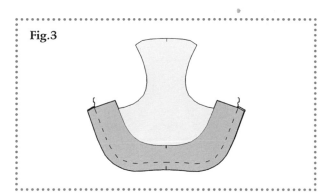

Fig.3

2 Overlap one side head over the curve of the upper head by 0.5cm (¼in) so that the right angle on the side head matches up to the seam on the flews. Oversew (or machine zigzag) the pieces together using a thread colour to match the side head. Repeat to attach the remaining side head to the opposite side of the upper head (**Fig.4**).

Fig.4

3 With right sides together, match the back head pieces along the notched edge and backstitch (or machine sew) together (**Fig.5**), then finger press the seam open.

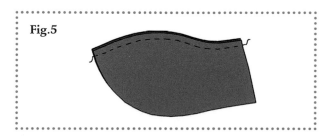

Fig.5

4 Matching the notches on the edge of the lower jaw piece, backstitch (or machine sew) to the dart points on each side (**Fig.6**). Push the dart bulk towards the centre front.

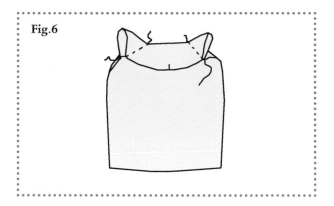

Fig.6

5 With the joined front/side heads right side facing up, position the lower jaw on top, right facing down, as shown in **Fig.7**. Match the centre front notches and start pinning the lower jaw edge to the free edge of the flews.

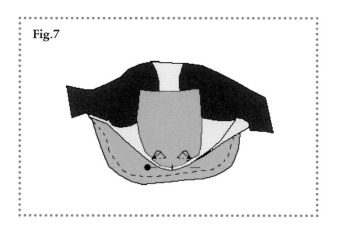

Fig.7

6 Starting from the centre front, either machine stitch or oversew by hand along one side, then sew the other side in the same way (**Fig.8**). This stitching won't be seen on the finished pup, so don't worry about tidiness here.

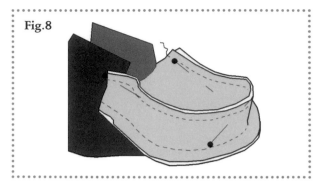

Fig.8

7 Push everything to be right sides out. Sew the buttons for the eyes in place. Roll the flew seams to the edge again. Moving the lower jaw out of the way, position the curved edge of the nose piece onto the head, leaving a 1cm (³/₈in) overhang and oversew in place using black thread (**Fig.9**).

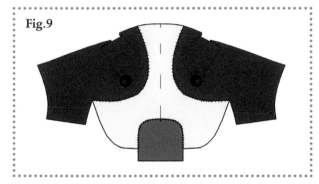

Fig.9

8 Roll up the 4cm (1½in) x 1cm (³/₈in) strip of black felt and slipstitch the free edge down to make a roll. Position centrally on the back of the nose overhang and slipstitch in place (**Fig.10**). Fold up and sew each side of the nose overhang to the underside of the flews using a double thread (**Fig.10**, detail), and keep a long thread for the next stage.

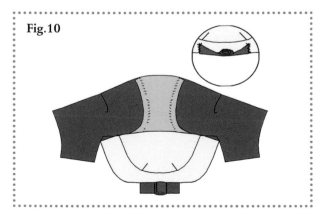

Fig.10

9 Turn the head over (right side facing up) and fold the nose down on itself on either side of the padded centre, creating three defined nose sections (**Fig. 11**). Once you have achieved this, sew through all folds, pulling the nose in slightly, passing the needle through a few times. Fasten off, and push the lower jaw out a little so it sits visibly under the nose.

Fig.11

10 Working on the inside of the back of the jaw, fold the flew and jaw layers so they sit smoothly against the side head. Pin, then sew through the layers, thereby controlling the shape of the head (**Fig.12**: left-hand image, shows roughly the position of the stitching but from the *outside*, and your stitching won't be visible if you work on the inside, as in the right-hand image).

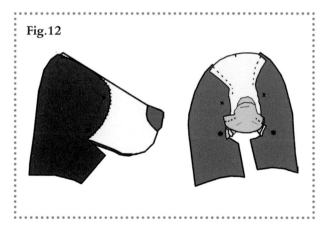

Fig.12

11 Take the ears and, with the ear stitching visible, position them with the folded edge on the outside, matching the stitched ear corner with the side head seam. Tack (baste) in place 0.5cm (¼in) from the top edge (**Fig.13**).

Fig.13

14 Tack (baste) a 1cm (³⁄₈in) seam allowance to the wrong side of the neckline, all the way around. Overlap the two remaining free edges of the side heads, taking each edge over to meet the other side of the lower jaw, and oversew together to finish the neck (**Fig.16**). Then sew the top of the overlapped pieces onto the back of the lower jaw (**Fig.17**).

12 With right sides together and the ears tucked in, match and pin the front head to the back head. Starting at the centre and sewing one side at a time, backstitch (or machine sew) around the head shape (**Fig.14**).

Fig.16

Fig.14

Fig.17

13 Turn the head through to the right side, pulling the ears out first (**Fig.15**). At this stage the ears look a little crazy!

15 Stuff the head through the neck opening but be careful not to stuff too compactly. On the muzzle part, make sure to only stuff into the lower jaw leaving the flews unstuffed.

Fig.15

Making the Body

1 Match the two side body pieces and, starting at the top point, sew approximately 4cm (1½in) down the back seam and then fasten off. Leaving an opening of 6cm (2³/₈in), resume sewing again until you reach the snip or notch at the base (**Fig.18**: left-hand image). Now match and pin the tummy panel to the edge of one of the back pieces, and sew all the way from the top point to where the notches meet. Repeat with the remaining tummy/back seam (**Fig.18**: right-hand image).

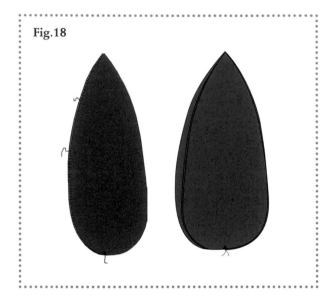

Fig.18

2 Stuff the body through the opening. When you are happy with the body shape, oversew the opening to close.

3 Check you have enough stuffing in the head, but still a gap for the point of the body cone to go in. Push the point of the body cone into the head. Pin to secure position. Using a medium-size darner needle and double thread, securely sew the head to the body using slip stitch, going around the neck at least twice.

Making the Legs

1 Oversew two leg pieces together along the long back seam, starting at the foot and finishing about 3.5cm (1³/₈in) past the curve at the top. Then starting from the front of the foot, sew up the front seam to just above the foot (**Fig.19**).

Fig.19

2 Now turn the foot part of the leg so that these seams are to the inside and pin the footpad in place, matching the notches on the footpad with the seams you have just sewn. Ease the footpad in place and sew all the way around using backstitch (**Fig.20**).

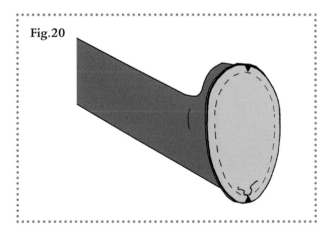

Fig.20

3 Turn the foot back out so that the raw edges of the felt are enclosed and stuff the foot firmly.

4 Resume oversewing the front leg seam, stuffing the leg firmly as you go. Now stuff the top curve of the leg but before you make it too full, push the components of a self-cover button together, then push it inside the stuffed leg so that the shank part is facing the felt, and the domed part is resting against some stuffing. The shank should be about 1.5cm (⁵/₈in) down from the highest part of the leg (roughly where the X is marked on the pattern).

5 Use a safety pin on the outside of the felt to secure the shank in place (**Fig.21**). Continue to stuff until firm and finish sewing all the way around. Repeat steps 1–5 to make the second leg, making sure that the shank is facing inwards to make an opposite leg.

Fig.21

6 Thread a long needle with elastic thread. Cut the end of the elastic at an angle to create a pointed end to go through the needle eye when threading. Pull the ends through so they are equal. Pass the threaded needle through the shank of the self-cover button in one leg (remove the safety pin). Push the needle through the body at the marked position so that it comes out at the same position on the other side. (You will have to compress the body so the needle comes out the other side.) Pass the needle through the shank of the self-cover button on the other leg and then pass the needle through the body again to the first side. Finally, go through the shank of the first leg again (**Fig.22**).

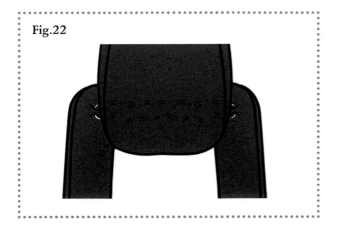

Fig.22

7 Pull both ends of elastic firmly and steadily to draw the legs into the body. When there is enough tension to pull the body in and make the leg tops seem to sit in the sockets, knot the ends of the elastic together at least three times. Check that everything is secure, then trim the elastic closely so that the ends disappear between the leg and the body.

Making the Arms
1 Follow the instructions in How to Make Luna for how to sew and attach Hugh's arms.

Making the Tail
1 Lay the contrast (white) tail tip over the main (brown) tail piece so that the edges match. Oversew in place along the inner seam (**Fig.23**). Once this is secure, you can cut away the excess main felt from underneath.

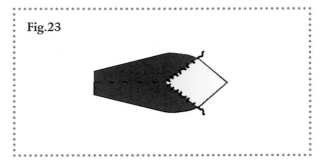

Fig.23

2 Now fold the tail in half lengthwise and oversew along the edge, switching threads to match the felt colours and allowing an opening for stuffing.

3 Stuff the tail gently to make it a little 3D (not too much though). Oversew the opening to close once you are happy. To attach the tail, sew onto the back of the body about 6cm (2³⁄₈in) up from the seam intersection.

FINISHING OFF

1 This step is completely optional. You can cut some softly curved patches out of the remaining contrast (white) felt and sew onto Hugh's body using slip stitch.

How to Make Rowan

YOU WILL NEED

- 23cm (9in) x 90cm (36in) main felt (ember)
- 11cm (4½in) x 20cm (8in) contrast felt (snow white)
- 10cm (4in) square of 100% cotton print fabric
- 24cm (9½in) x 30cm (12in) faux fur fabric
- Scrap of black felt
- Two 10mm (³⁄₈in) buttons for eyes and two 15mm (⁵⁄₈in) buttons for arm joints
- Two 20mm (¾in) press studs
- Toy stuffing about 150gm (5¼oz)
- Basic sewing kit (see Materials)

Use a 0.5cm (¼in) seam allowance, unless a different amount is stated.

CUTTING OUT

1 Pin the cut-out pattern pieces (see Patterns) onto the main (ember) felt (partially folded), using the layout in **Fig.1** as a guide and noting which pieces should be cut in which colour. Pin the relevant pieces onto single layer contrast (white) felt. Cut the pieces out and mark any triangles or notches with a tiny snip in the felt. Transfer all other pattern markings using tailor's tacks or a water-soluble pen.

Fig.1

2 Pin the cut-out pattern pieces for the tail (see Patterns) onto the wrong side of the faux fur fabric using the layout in **Fig.2** as a guide and cut out. Mark notches as before and transfer any other pattern markings.

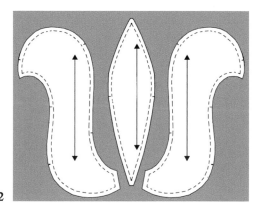

Fig.2

3 Cut out a pair of footpads from the cotton print fabric marking triangles with a snip as before.

MAKING UP

Making the Ears

1 Position a white inner ear flash onto a main ear piece and oversew using white thread, making sure that your stitches don't show on the back. Repeat to make the second ear, a mirror image of the first (**Fig.3**).

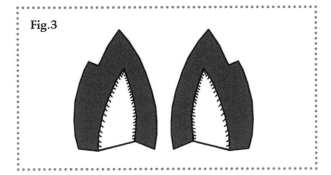

Fig.3

2 Fold the ear edges inwards and over the inner ear flashes at the notches, and tack (baste) the layers together 0.5cm (¼in) up from the lower edge (**Fig.4**). Working on a protective surface, use a needle to draw the fibres outwards at the top point of the ear for a soft, fluffy edge.

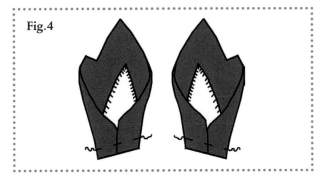

Fig.4

Making the Head

1 With the side head pieces placed so that the rounded bits (the cheek pouches) are facing towards you and the necks facing inwards, place an ear on each seam extension (top of head) with the inner ear flashes facing downwards. Following **Fig.5** as a guide, centre the ears on the seam extension and tack (baste) in place.

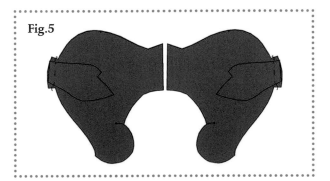

Fig.5

2 Working on one side at a time, place the head gusset with the more rounded end pointing towards the nose, matching the seam extension to that of the side head, sandwiching the ear in between (**Fig.6**). Backstitch or (machine sew) through all layers (**Fig.7**).

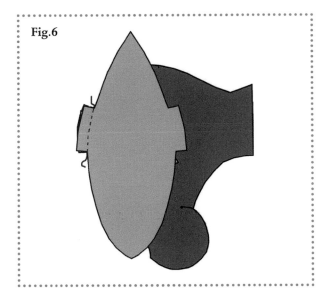

Fig.6

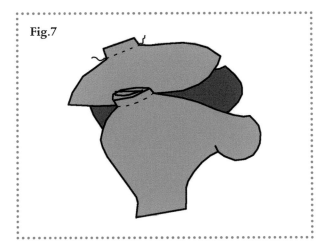

Fig.7

3 Working on one side at a time, oversew from the front of the ear to join head gusset to side head (**Fig.8**).

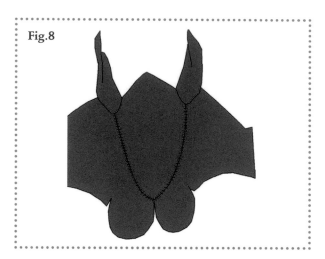

Fig.8

4 Now oversew from the back of the ear to the notch that indicates where the gusset ends (**Fig.9**).

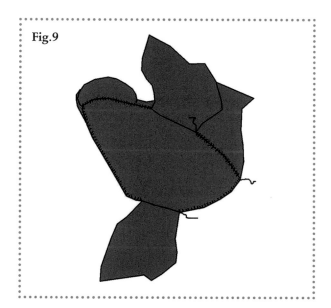

Fig.9

5 Starting at the point where the curve has been cut into the side head, sew with a short running stitch about 0.2cm (^{3}/$_{32}$in) away from the edge around the curve. Leave the long tail of thread on the wrong side and don't fasten off. Using a new length of thread, sew with a running stitch back along the curved shape, this time 0.4cm (^{5}/$_{32}$in) away from the edge and again leaving a long tail of thread on the wrong side (**Fig.10**).

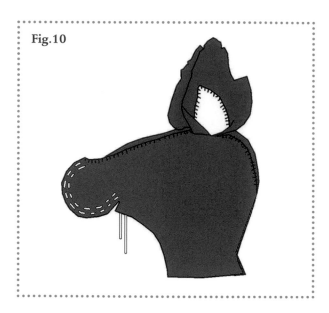

Fig.10

6 Use the thread tails to gather up the stitches to create a curved shape that you can push your little fingertip into. When you are happy with the pouch shape of the cheek, tie the thread ends to one another (**Fig.11**). Repeat to create the cheek pouch on the other side of the head.

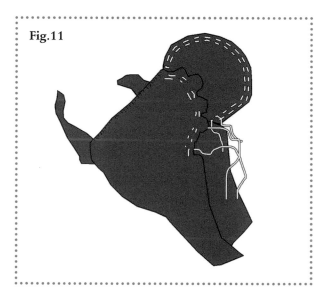

Fig.11

7 Working on one side at a time, take the pouch and overlap it onto the side head (**Fig.12**), so the curve comes down the jawline by about 0.5cm (¼in). Sew securely in place (**Fig.13**).

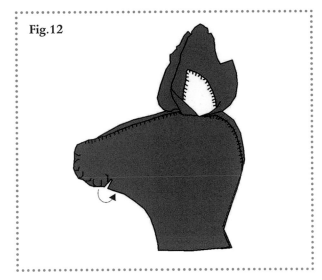

Fig.12

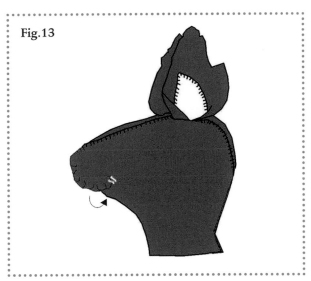

Fig.13

9 Using the guide stitchlines on the throat pattern, oversew the throat piece securely at the front of the head, so it sits behind the main colour with a 0.5cm (¼in) overlap at each side with the base of the cheek pouches sitting level to the guide stitchline at the top (**Fig.15**).

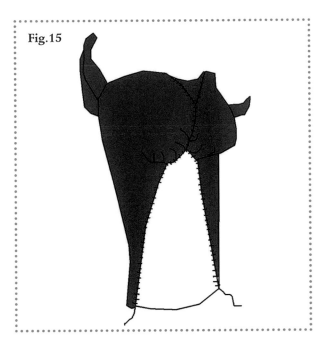

Fig.15

10 Match up the back head seam below where the gusset finishes and oversew together down to the lower neck, fastening off securely (**Fig.16**).

8 Sew the front edges of the nose together from the nose tip – approx. 1cm (³/₈in) (**Fig.14**).

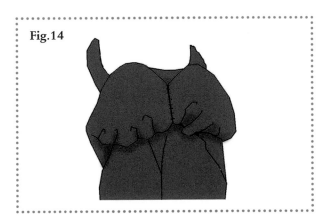

Fig.14

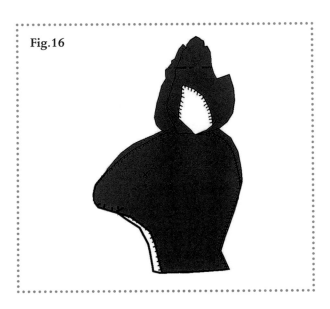

Fig.16

11 Turn the 1cm (³⁄₈in) neck seam allowance up inside the head. Stuff the head through the neck opening, pushing stuffing into the cheek pouches and nose area. Fill the head, making sure the seam allowances for the ears are sitting towards the side heads to enable the ears to be more upright. You will come back to the head once you have constructed the body, as the stuffing may have settled and you may need to add more later. Position the black felt nose triangle centrally on the cheek pouch area, using **Fig.17** as a guide, and sew in place.

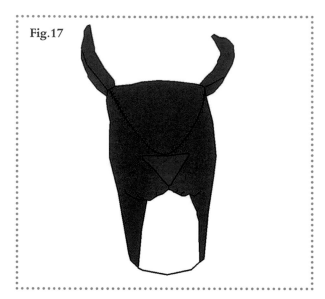

Fig.17

Making the Legs
1 Follow the instructions in How to Make Luna for how to sew and attach Rowan's legs.

Making the Body
1 Follow the instructions in How to Make Luna for how to sew Rowan's body, making sure the contrast panel is the one that is inbetween the other two body panels, therefore becoming the tummy panel. The legs will be positioned onto the tummy panel.

Making the Arms
1 Follow the instructions in How to Make Luna for how to sew and attach Rowan's arms.

Making the Tail
1 With right sides together, sew the two side tails together along the centre back seam, leaving an opening between the notches. Sew up the top of the tail to the marked dot. Sew the upper edges together at the lower end, between the marked dots (**Fig.18**).

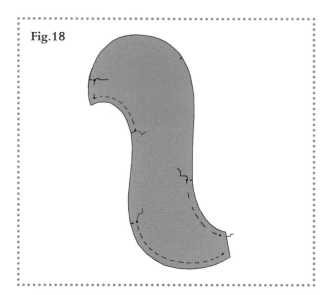

Fig.18

2 Working on one side at a time, match the tail gusset to the side tail and sew between the notches (**Fig.19**).

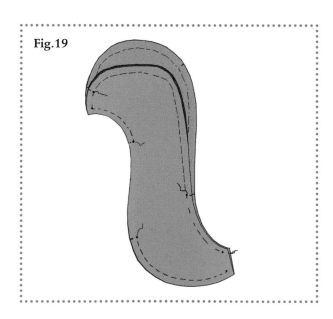

Fig.19

3 Flatten the short end of the tail so the seams match, then sew across (**Fig.20**). Trim excess fabric at the corners and turn through to the right side. Stuff the tail, ensuring you work the stuffing into the upper end. Leave 2cm (¾in) of the lower end of the tail unstuffed, where it will sit under the base.

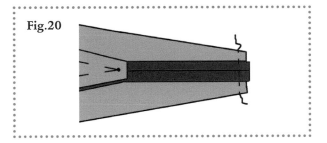

Fig.20

FINISHING OFF

1 Rowan's tail is attached to her body with press studs making it removable so that she can enjoy a wearing a larger selection of clothes! Trim the fur pile away where press studs are to be positioned and sew on securely with double thread. Sew one half of the first press stud on the seam, 1cm (⅜in) from the short end of the tail facing upwards. Sew the other half onto the body base – in line with the centre back – about 1cm (⅜in) from the seam. Holding the tail up against Rowan's head and body, judge where the second press stud should go. First sew half of the press stud to the centre of the tail gusset, then sew the other half onto the back of Rowan's body in the vicinity of the neck.

2 Position the button eyes according to the pattern and sew on in the same way as you did the arms, passing the needle through from one side of the face to the other, applying a little tension to pull the eyes in slightly and shape the head (**Fig.21**).

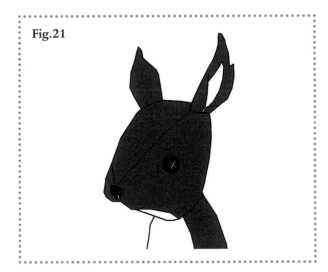

Fig.21

How to Make Daisy

YOU WILL NEED

- **23cm (9in) x 38cm (15in) main felt (snow white)**
- **16.5cm (6½in) x 90cm (36in) contrast felt (grey)**
- **Two 10mm (³/₈in) buttons for eyes and three 15mm (⁵/₈in) buttons for arm joints**
- **Toy stuffing about 120gm (4½oz)**
- **Two 20mm (¾in) self-cover buttons**
- **1m (39in) of 0.8mm elastic thread**
- **1m (39in) of textured yarn**
- **Six-stranded embroidery cotton (floss) in black for facial features**
- **Basic sewing kit (see Materials)**

Use a 0.5cm (¼in) seam allowance, unless a different amount is stated.

CUTTING OUT

1 Pin the cut-out pattern pieces (see Patterns) onto the main (white) felt (partially folded), using the layout in **Fig.1** as a guide and noting which pieces should be cut in which colour. Pin the relevant pieces onto the contrast (grey) felt (partially folded), using the layout in **Fig.2** as a guide. Cut the pieces out and mark any triangles or notches with a tiny snip in the felt. Transfer all other pattern markings using tailor's tacks or a water-soluble pen.

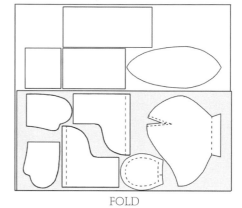

Fig.1

FOLD

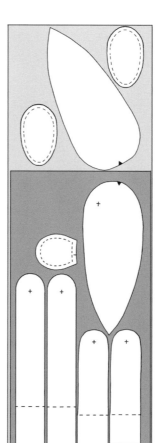

Fig.2

FOLD

MAKING UP

Making the Ears

1 Match one outer (main felt) ear piece to an inner (contrast felt) ear piece and sew around the curved edge using a backstitch (or machine sew), leaving the bottom (notched) edge open. Trim the seam allowance to 0.3cm (¹⁄₈in), then turn through to the right side. Roll the seams out to the edge and press flat with a warm iron (**Fig.3**). Repeat to make a second ear, making sure it is a mirror image of the first.

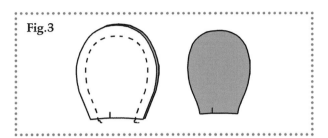

Fig.3

2 Working on one ear at a time, fold the ear over at the notch so that the contrast felt is to the inside, making sure that the lower edges match. Tack (baste) or pin to keep in place (**Fig.4**). The ears should be a mirror image of each other.

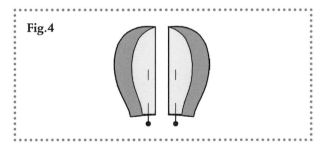

Fig.4

Making the Head

1 Snip to the dot as marked on each side head piece (**Fig.5**).

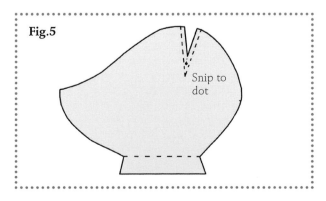

Fig.5

Snip to dot

2 With the side head pieces facing one another, place a folded ear on each so that the contrast (grey) felt is facing downwards and the folded edge of the ear is towards the top of the head, with the bottom of the ear sitting tight to the end of the snip. Make sure that the short edge of the ear matches the edge of the head dart with 0.5cm (¼in) of felt visible above the ear (**Fig.6**). When you are happy, pin in place.

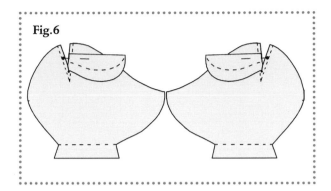

Fig.6

3 Fold the back of the side head piece over to enclose the ear, matching up the edges of the dart. Making sure that the ear is still tucked right up to the snip point, backstitch or machine sew (machine is easier) through all layers at a depth of 0.3cm (¹⁄₈in) at the top edge, tapering to nothing just below the snip dot (**Fig.7**). Repeat on the other side head piece.

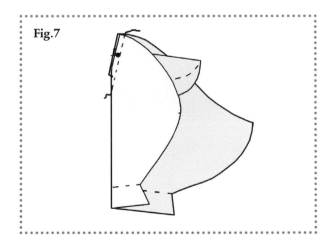

Fig.7

4 Match the side head pieces with the ears to the outside and oversew from the front neck edge to the nose point (**Fig.8**).

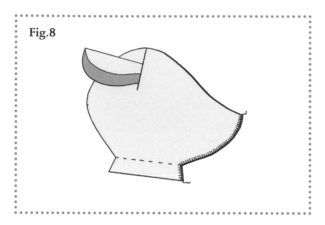

Fig.8

5 Match the gusset along one side of the head, making sure you have the wider end of the gusset at the front. Oversew in place, finishing where the back point of the gusset matches the snip, then continue around to join the gusset to the other side of the head. At the ears, make sure the dart seam allowance is tucked in and just catch the outer edge. Finish invisibly on the wrong side at the nose (**Fig.9**).

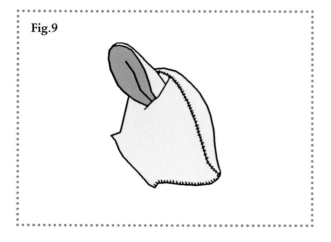

Fig.9

6 Match up the back head seam below where the gusset finishes and sew together down to the lower neck, fastening off securely (**Fig.10**). Stuff the head through the neck opening using small pieces of stuffing to build up the shape to be full and round. Turn the 1cm (³⁄₈in) neck seam allowance up inside the head. You will come back to the head once you have constructed the body, so the stuffing may have settled and you may need to add more later.

Fig.10

7 Fold tuft strip 1 in half lengthwise and pin close to the folded edge. Make snips all along the unfolded edges about 0.5cm (¼in) apart and stopping 0.5cm (¼in) from the folded edge. Keeping the fold in place, use a double thread to sew a line of running stitch through both layers, leaving a long tail of thread (**Fig.11**). Gather the strip up slightly until the width matches the distance between the ears.

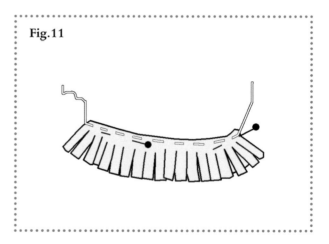

Fig.11

8 With the front of the head facing away from you, pin the long-tailed side of the prepared tuft strip to the left-hand side just inside the head gusset seam. Adjust the gathering to fit if necessary, then sew the right-hand side down securely, continuing to slip stitch the fold of the strip onto the head gusset. When you get to the other end tie the gathering threads off to finish (**Fig.12**).

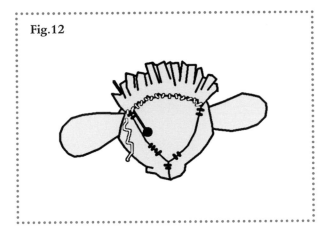

Fig.12

11 To embroider the nose and the mouth, refer to **Fig.14** and **Fig 15**. Using all six strands of the black embroidery thread, tie a knot in the end and bring the needle up through the inside of the head from the neck opening to a point just below the nose at A. Travel 1.5cm ($^5/_8$in) to B, and take a small stitch under the seam to come out at C on the head gusset, then travel to D on the opposite side of the head gusset. Take a small stitch under the seam to come out at E (directly opposite B). Travel back to A and take a small stitch trying to keep at the centre. Now pass your needle under the horizontal thread (at C–D) and bring it down to F, 1cm ($^3/_8$in) below the nose. Take a 1cm ($^3/_8$in) long stitch to G to come back out at F, then repeat to H to come back out at F again. Fasten off with a couple of tiny stitches at F, then bring your needle back out through the head to finish.

9 Repeat steps 6 and 7 to prepare and attach tuft strips 2 and 3, leaving about 1.5cm ($^5/_8$in) between each strip, to virtually fill the back of the head gusset (**Fig.13**). Randomly trim the tufts to give a natural appearance, making the tufts near the ears shorter to create a dome shape over the head.

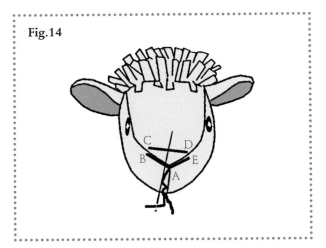

Fig.14

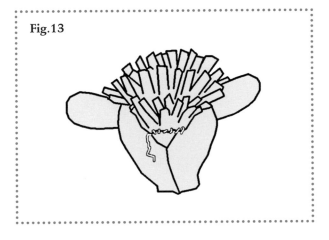

Fig.13

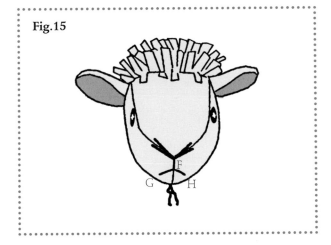

Fig.15

10 Position the button eyes according to the pattern and sew on in the same way as you will the arms (see Making the Arms), passing the needle through from one side of the face to the other, but without pulling the head shape in.

Making the Legs

1 Oversew the foot pieces to the leg pieces (**Fig.16**). Remember you will be making two mirrored pairs. From now on the leg pieces have a right and a wrong side.

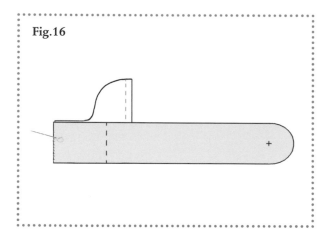

Fig.16

2 Bring the seam up on each leg piece to meet the dashed line on the leg pattern and press flat. Pin, then invisibly sew through all layers just below the line of overstitching (**Fig.17**). This creates a flap of folded felt on the right side of the leg.

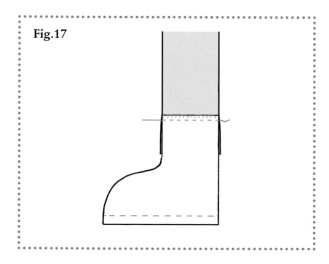

Fig.17

3 With right sides together, match two leg pieces and oversew along the long back seam, starting at the foot and finishing about 3.5cm (1³/₈in) past the curve at the top, changing threads to match the felt and keeping the folded part free of the seam. Then, starting from the foot, sew the front seam up to just before the curve of the foot (**Fig.18**).

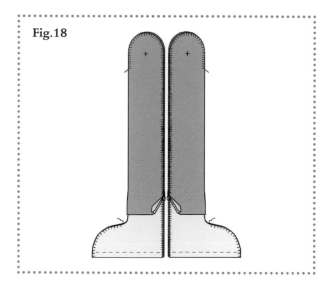

Fig.18

4 Now turn the foot part of the leg so that these seams are to the inside and pin the footpad in place, matching the notches on the footpad with the seams you have just sewn. Ease the footpad in place and sew all the way around using backstitch (**Fig.19**).

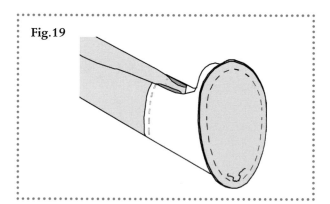

Fig.19

5 Turn the foot back out so that the raw edges of the felt are enclosed and stuff the foot firmly.

6 Resume oversewing the front leg seam, stuffing the leg firmly as you go. Stuff the top curve of the leg but before you make it too full, push the components of a self-cover button together, then push it inside the stuffed leg so that the shank part is facing the felt and the domed part is resting against some stuffing. It should be about 1.5cm (⁵/₈in) down from the highest part of the leg (see X marked on pattern). Use a safety pin on the outside of the felt to secure the shank in place (**Fig.21**). Continue to stuff until firm and finish sewing all the way around. Repeat steps to make the second leg, making sure that the shank is facing inwards to make an opposite leg.

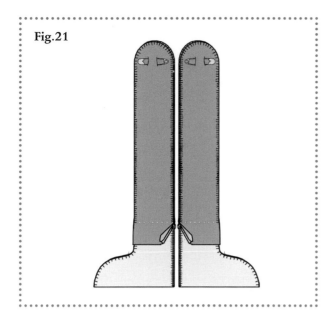

Fig.21

Fig.23

7 Using a small pair of scissors, cut through the folded felt 'cuff' to within 0.5cm (¼in) of the stitching, creating loops that are just a little less than 0.5cm (¼in) wide. Then snip through each loop at different levels and angles to create an uneven layered look to the tufts (**Fig.22**).

Making the Arms

1 Oversew the hand pieces to the arm pieces (**Fig.24**). Remember you will be making two mirrored pairs. From now on the arm pieces have a right and a wrong side.

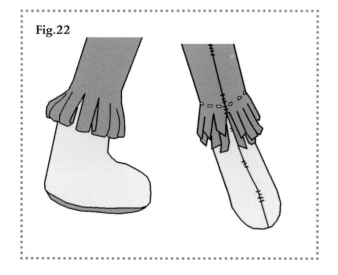

Fig.22

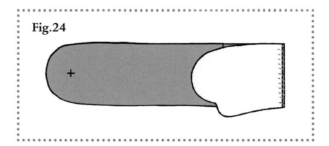

Fig.24

2 Bring the seam up on each arm piece to meet the dashed line on the arm pattern and press flat. Pin, then invisibly sew through all layers just below the line of overstitching (**Fig.25**). This creates a flap of folded felt on the right side of the arm.

Making the Body

1 Follow the instructions in How to Make Hugh for how to sew Daisy's body. When sewing on the head with slip stitch, I tend to go around fairly loosely on round one and then tighten up in round two, three, four – after all, no one wants a headless creature (**Fig.23**).

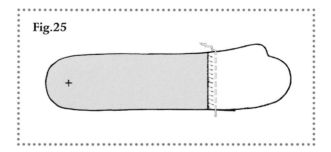

Fig.25

3 With right sides together, match two arm pieces and oversew starting at the back of the arm, over the arm top and down to the front of the hand. Use a deeper stitch to define the thumb, then continue, stopping 4cm (1½in) from where you started. Remember to change threads to match the felt, and also to keep the folded part free of the seam. Stuff the arm firmly and then sew the opening closed. Repeat to make a second arm (**Fig.26**). Cut into the folded felt 'cuffs' exactly as you did on the legs.

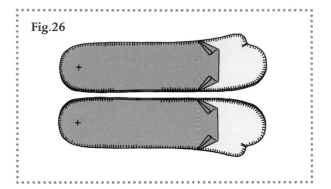

Fig.26

Attaching the Arms and Legs

1 To attach the arms to the body, follow the instructions for How to Make Luna: Making the Arms, step 3.

2 To attach the legs to the body, follow the instructions for How to Make Hugh: Making the Body, steps 6 and 7 (**Fig.27**).

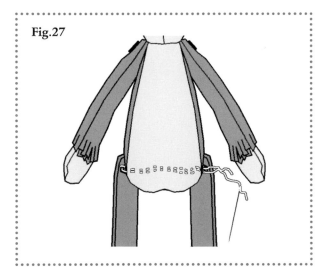

Fig.27

Making the Tail

1 Wrap the yarn around three fingers, four times. Slip the yarn off your fingers and pinch the loops together as you wind the tail around the strands, to leave a bunch of loops extending about 1.5cm (⅝in) at the top and 2.5cm (2in) at the bottom (**Fig.28**).

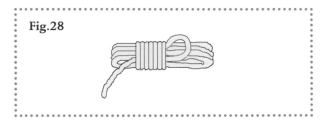

Fig.28

2 Thread the tail through a large-eyed needle and pass it through the bound section to fasten off. Snip through the long loops at the bottom to make a tassel (**Fig.29**).

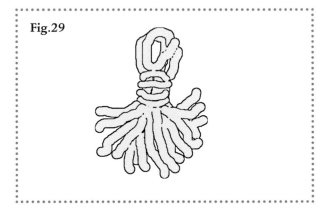

Fig.29

3 Sew the tail onto the centre back body seam with the top being about 7cm (2¾in) from the three seam intersection.

YOU WILL NEED

- **Refer to Daisy You Will Need for your requirements.**

Use a 0.5cm (¼in) seam allowance, unless a different amount is stated.

CUTTING OUT

1 Pin the cut-out pattern pieces (see Patterns) onto the main (white) felt (partially folded), referring to the Fig.1 layout for Daisy as a guide and noting which pieces should be cut in which colour. Pin the relevant pieces onto the contrast (grey) felt (partially folded), using the layout in **Fig.1** below as a guide. Cut the pieces out and mark any triangles or notches with a tiny snip in the felt. Transfer all other pattern markings using tailor's tacks or a water-soluble pen.

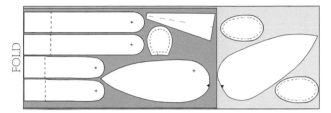

Fig.1

MAKING UP

Making the Ears

1 Follow the instructions in How to Make Daisy for how to sew and attach Ramsey's ears.

Making the Horns

1 Thread a needle with double black thread and fasten on the thread to the inside of the narrow end of the wedge-shaped horn piece. Pull the thread out so it is usable and fold in half lengthways (**Fig.2**).

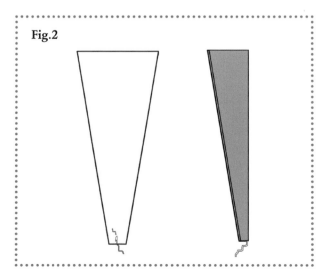

Fig.2

2 Sew up the unfolded side with blanket stitch, making your stitches about 0.5cm (¼in) deep and the same distance apart. Pull each stitch tight so the shape starts to curl and the stitches sink in. Finish about 1cm (³⁄₈in) from the end (**Fig.3**).

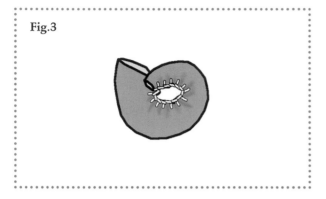

Fig.3

3 Repeat to make second horn, manipulating it so the curve is a mirror image of the first horn.

Making the Head

1 Follow the instructions in How to Make Daisy: Making the Head, steps 1 and 2, for how to sew Ramsey's head. Then pop the horns over the ears, making sure they don't come above the top of the head pieces, deepening the snip into the head if necessary (**Fig.4**). Continue with the remaining steps in How to Make Daisy to complete Ramsey's head.

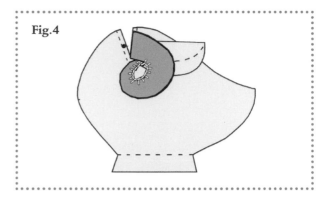

Fig.4

Making the Legs, Body and Arms

1 Follow the instructions in How to Make Daisy for how to sew Ramsey's legs, body and arms.

Attaching the Arms and Legs

1 Follow the instructions in How to Make Daisy for how to attach Ramsey's arms and legs.

Making the Tail

1 Follow the instructions in How to Make Daisy for how to sew Ramsey's tail.

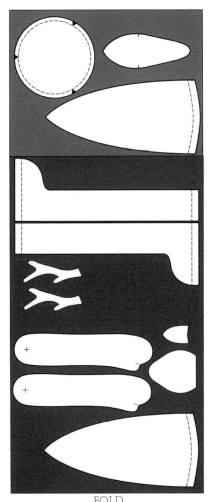

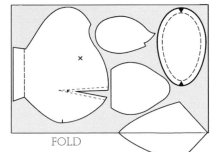

YOU WILL NEED

- 21cm (8½in) x 90cm (36in) main felt (camel)
- 23cm (9in) x 20cm (8in) contrast felt (white)
- Scrap of black felt for the nose, tail and eyes
- 10cm (4in) x 18cm (7in) medium-weight iron-on interfacing
- Two 10mm (3/8in) buttons for eyes and two 15mm (⁵/₈in) buttons for arm joints
- Toy stuffing about 120gm (4½oz)
- Basic sewing kit (see Materials)

Use a 0.5cm (¼in) seam allowance, unless a different amount is stated.

CUTTING OUT

1 Pin the cut-out pattern pieces (see Patterns) onto the main (camel) felt (partially folded), using the layout in **Fig.1** as a guide and noting which pieces should be cut in which colour. Pin the relevant pieces onto the contrast (white) felt (folded in half), using the layout in **Fig.2** as a guide. Cut the pieces out and mark any triangles or notches with a tiny snip in the felt. Transfer all other pattern markings using tailor's tacks or a water-soluble pen. Keep all scraps of the white felt for adding the needlefelt decorative details later.

Fig.1

FOLD

Fig.2

FOLD

How to Make Freya

MAKING UP

Making the Ears

1 Match an inner (main felt – camel) ear piece to an outer (contrast felt – white) ear piece using the centre notches and sew in place about 0.2cm (³/₃₂in) from the edge using double white thread and a short running stitch. Sew two more lines of decorative stitching following the shape of the inner ear (**Fig.3**). Repeat to make a second ear piece.

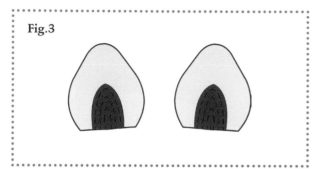

Fig.3

2 With right sides together, match a prepared ear piece from step 1 to one of the main felt (camel) outer ear pieces. Sew around the curved edge using backstitch (or machine sew), leaving the bottom (notched) edge open. Trim the seam allowance to 0.3cm (¹/₈in). Turn through to the right side (easiest done by pulling the sides apart at the widest point and then pushing the tip inwards). Roll the seam to the edge and press with a warm iron (**Fig.4**). Repeat to make a second ear.

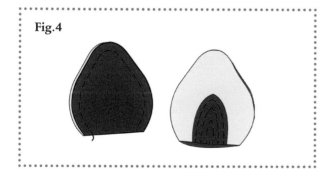

Fig.4

3 Fold one edge of the ear over to the centre notch (the bulk may mean that a tip of white will be the edge – rather than the seam – but that's fine). Repeat with the other ear so it is a mirror image of the first. Tack (baste) or pin at the lower edge to keep in place (**Fig.5**).

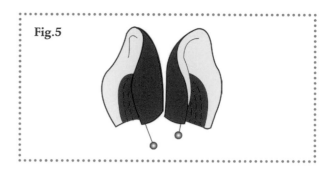

Fig.5

Making the Antlers

1 Fuse interfacing to one side of each of the antler pieces to give you two mirrored pairs.

2 Match two antler pieces with interfacing to the inside, and pin together. Sew together using a short decorative running stitch about 0.2cm (³/₃₂in) from the edge. Repeat to make the second antler, a mirror image of the first (**Fig.6**).

Fig.6

Making the Head

1 Snip to the dot as marked on each side head piece. With the side head pieces facing one another, place a folded ear on each so that the contrast (white) felt is facing downwards and the folded edge of the ear is towards the top of the head, with the bottom of the ear sitting tight to the end of the snip. Make sure that the short edge of the ear matches the edge of the head dart (**Fig.7**). When you are happy, pin in place.

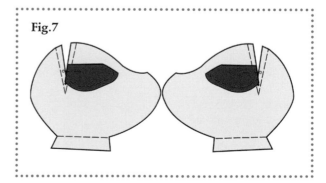

Fig.7

2 Place the antlers over the ears, making sure they don't come above the top of the head pieces (make sure there is still 0.3cm/⅛in of the head felt visible), deepening the snip into the head if necessary. Align the edge of the antler with the angle of the ear dart and make sure your best stitching will be showing the same way up as the right side of the ears (**Fig.8**).

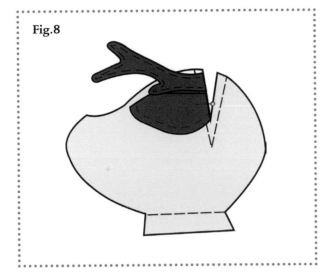

Fig.8

3 Fold the back of the side head piece over to enclose the ear/antler, matching up the edges of the dart. Making sure that the ear is still tucked right up to the snip point, backstitch or machine sew (machine is easier) through all layers at a depth of 0.3cm (⅛in) at the top edge, tapering to nothing just below the snip dot. Repeat on the other side head piece (**Fig.9**).

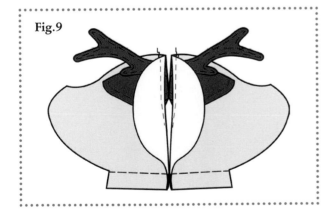

Fig.9

4 Match the side head pieces with the ears to the outside and oversew from the front neck edge to the nose point (**Fig.10**).

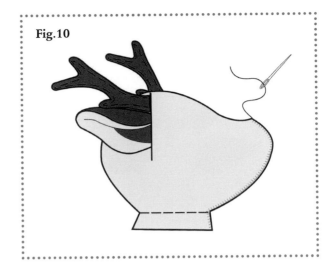

Fig.10

5 Match the gusset along one side of the head, making sure you have the narrower end of the gusset at the front. Oversew in place, finishing where the back point of the gusset matches the snip, then continue around to join the gusset to the other side of the head. At the ears, make sure the dart seam allowance is tucked in and just catch the outer edge. Finish invisibly on the wrong side at the nose (**Fig.11**).

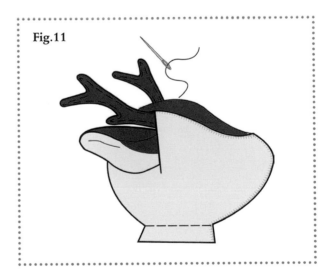

Fig.11

6 Match up the back head seam below where the gusset finishes and sew together down to the lower neck, fastening off securely (**Fig.12**). Stuff the head through the neck opening using small pieces of stuffing to build up the shape to be full and round. Turn the 1cm (⅜in) neck seam allowance up inside the head. You will come back to the head once you have constructed the body, so the stuffing may have settled and you may need to add more later.

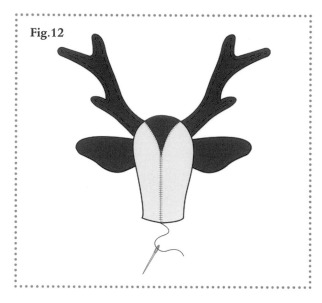

Fig.12

Fig.14

7 Take the black felt nose piece, fold it in half and sew a small pleat on each side about 0.4cm (⁵/₃₂in) in from each edge (your stitches should be about 0.2cm/³/₃₂in) deep). Turn through to the right side and push the nose shape out (**Fig.13**).

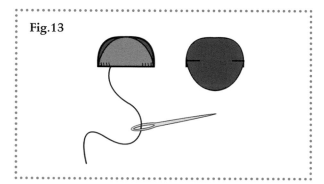

Fig.13

8 Oversew the nose in place with black thread following **Fig.14** as your guide. Position the button eyes according to the pattern. Using a long double thread and a long needle, sew the eyes onto the head, passing the needle through from one side of the face to the other, pulling the head shape in a tiny bit.

WARNING: BE CAREFUL WHEN USING THE FELTING NEEDLE IN STEP 9 AS IT IS EASY TO STAB YOURSELF! To needlefelt, stab the felt piece onto the main piece with a repetitive motion until you feel it is embedded. If the felting has caused a depression, push back to its original shape.

9 Referring back to **Fig.14**, push the uncut edge of one of the eyelash pieces tight under the outside edge of one of the buttons. When you are happy with the angle, use a felting needle to stab the shape into place just under the button (or sew down invisibly, if you prefer). Take some small pieces of felt roughly 0.5cm–0.7cm (¼in–⁹/₃₂in) square and use the felting needle to randomly felt them onto the head gusset.

Making the Legs

1 Follow the instructions in How to Make Luna for how to sew Freya's legs, using felt footpads rather than cotton ones.

Making the Body

1 Lay the contrast bib piece over the top of one of the body pieces (this now becomes the tummy). Oversew in place along the V shaped edge of the bib (**Fig.15**), then cut away the main felt beneath the bib to about 0.5cm (¼in) from the overstitching.

Fig.15

2 Follow the instructions in How to Make Luna: Making the Body, steps 1–4 for how to complete Freya's body, making sure the contrast bib panel is the one that is inbetween the other two body panels, therefore becoming the tummy panel. The legs will be positioned onto the tummy panel. Stuff the body, but leave it open for now and do not attach the head just yet.

Making the Arms

1 Follow the instructions in How to Make Luna for how to sew and attach Freya's arms.

Attaching the Head to the Body

1 Check you have enough stuffing in the head, but still a gap for the point of the body cone. Push the point of the body cone into the head. Using double thread and a medium-size darner needle, sew the head to the body using slip stitch and ensuring it is well attached by going around the neck at least twice (**Fig.16**). I tend to go around fairly loosely on round one and then tighten up in round two, three and four.

Making the Body Spots

1 You can use the needlefelt technique (see Making the Head, step 9) to randomly apply small pieces of felt – this time between 1cm–1.5cm (³⁄₈in–⁵⁄₈in) square – to make body spots all over the back of Freya's body. (We have also used a length of felting wool to create a soft line down the sides of the body but this is completely optional.)

2 Once the needlefelting is complete, finish stuffing the body and sew down the opening using slip stitch.

Making the Tail

1 Sew the black tail flash onto one of the tail pieces using lines of decorative running stitch. Match the tail pieces, so that the piece with the tail flash is facing outwards, and sew all the way around, leaving an opening on one side (**Fig.17**). Lightly stuff, then sew the opening closed.

2 Position the tail at the base of the centre back seam with the pointed end of the tail pointing upwards. Sew to secure the back layer to the body.

Fig.16

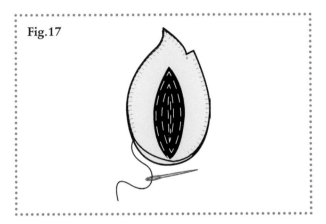

Fig.17

The Patterns

When using patterns follow these general guidelines:

- All pattern pieces are shown actual size so there is no need to reduce or enlarge. However, some may need to be joined with adhesive tape to complete the pattern piece so please follow the advice given.

- Refer to the pattern layout diagram with each project to see which patterns are needed.

- The patterns have seam allowances included. The allowances are stated in the project instructions.

- Before cutting out your pattern pieces from your fabric, iron the patterns and your fabric to remove any creases.

- Once copied, cut your paper patterns out first before you pin them onto the fabric. I like to cut on the black line, but to the outside not the inside.

- Some patterns only show half of the shape and these are clearly marked. In these cases, place the marked line along the fold of the fabric, so when the shape is cut out you will double the pattern.

- Cutting out is crucial to success so the use of pins when positioning a pattern on fabric will really improve your results. When pinning, keep the entire pin inside the pattern so there is no danger of your scissors hitting the pin.

- Grainlines – placing your pattern pieces on the grainline of fabric helps the pattern pieces keep their shape. The grainline of a fabric is parallel to the selvedges – the finished edges of a piece of fabric. For these tiny garments try to follow our layouts as we have placed the shapes along the grainline, but on this scale of things it's not going to make or break your garment.

You will see symbols on the patterns – some of the common ones are shown and explained here.

⟷ Straight grain of fabric

– – – Sewing line

▼ | ● Triangle/notch and dot position markers

⤬ Buttonhole, button and press stud positions

▼——▼ Place on fold of fabric

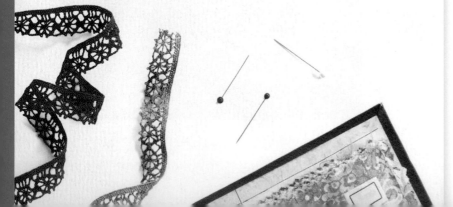

SHARED BODY PARTS

In this section you will find patterns relevant to more than one animal, so do take note of the pieces and cutting requirements relevant to the character you are making. Each character also has unique pattern pieces and you will find these in the Unique Body Parts section that follows.

ARM

LUNA, HUGH, ROWAN, FREYA
Cut 4 in main felt

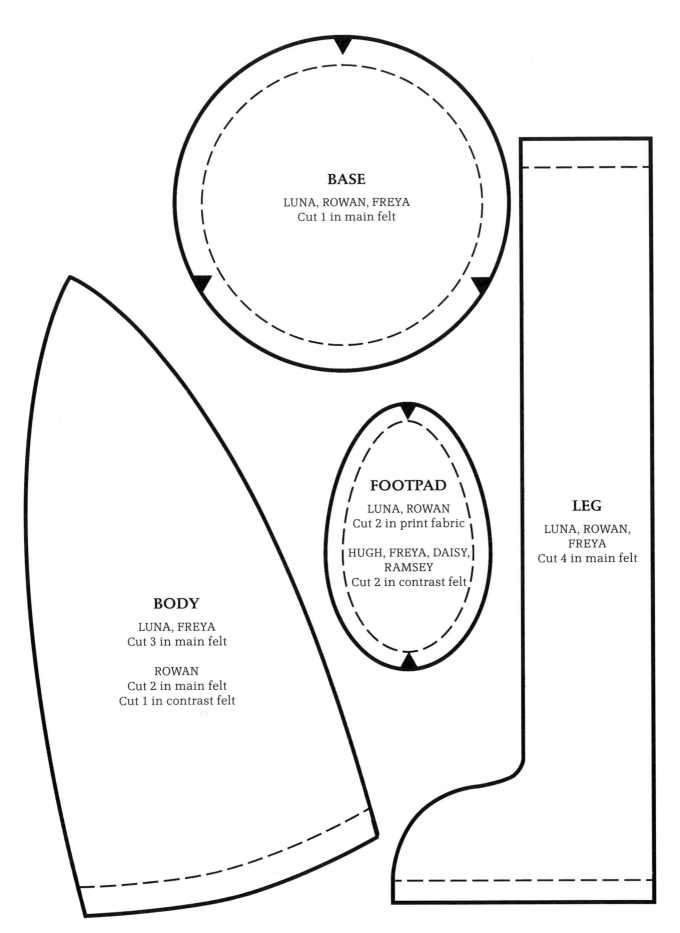

BASE

LUNA, ROWAN, FREYA
Cut 1 in main felt

LEG

LUNA, ROWAN,
FREYA
Cut 4 in main felt

FOOTPAD

LUNA, ROWAN
Cut 2 in print fabric

HUGH, FREYA, DAISY,
RAMSEY
Cut 2 in contrast felt

BODY

LUNA, FREYA
Cut 3 in main felt

ROWAN
Cut 2 in main felt
Cut 1 in contrast felt

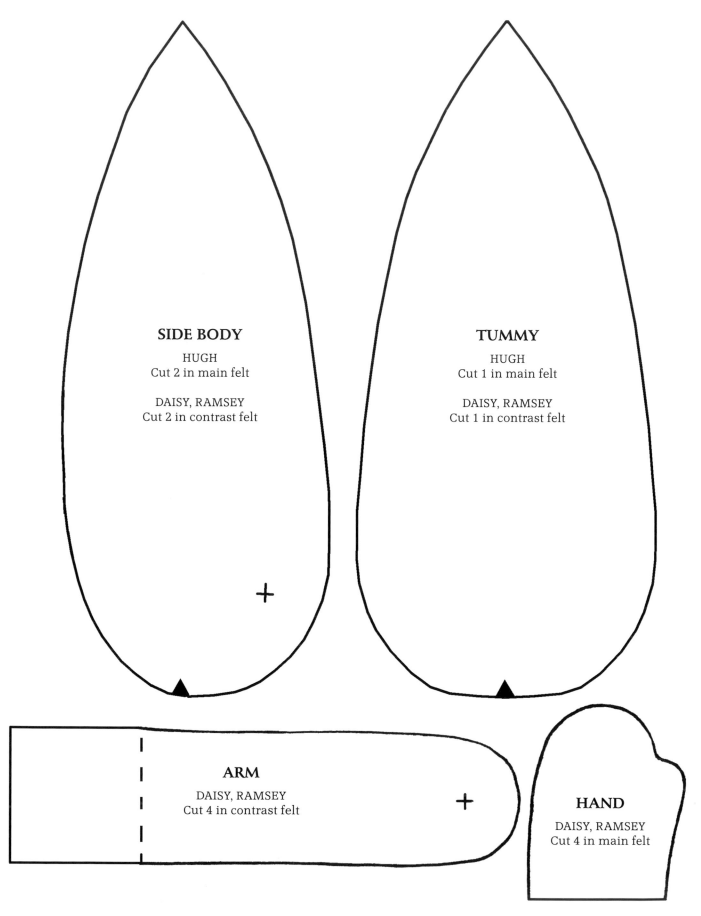

SIDE BODY

HUGH
Cut 2 in main felt

DAISY, RAMSEY
Cut 2 in contrast felt

TUMMY

HUGH
Cut 1 in main felt

DAISY, RAMSEY
Cut 1 in contrast felt

ARM

DAISY, RAMSEY
Cut 4 in contrast felt

HAND

DAISY, RAMSEY
Cut 4 in main felt

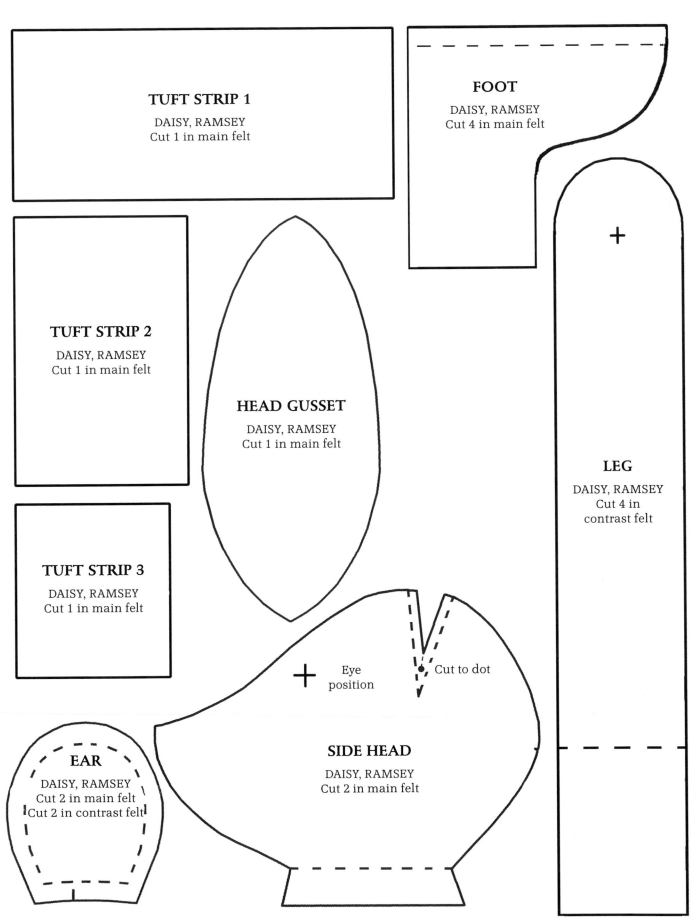

TUFT STRIP 1

DAISY, RAMSEY
Cut 1 in main felt

FOOT

DAISY, RAMSEY
Cut 4 in main felt

TUFT STRIP 2

DAISY, RAMSEY
Cut 1 in main felt

HEAD GUSSET

DAISY, RAMSEY
Cut 1 in main felt

LEG

DAISY, RAMSEY
Cut 4 in
contrast felt

TUFT STRIP 3

DAISY, RAMSEY
Cut 1 in main felt

Eye
position

Cut to dot

SIDE HEAD

DAISY, RAMSEY
Cut 2 in main felt

EAR

DAISY, RAMSEY
Cut 2 in main felt
Cut 2 in contrast felt

UNIQUE BODY PARTS

In this section you will find patterns unique to each animal as well as patterns for all the clothes and accessories.

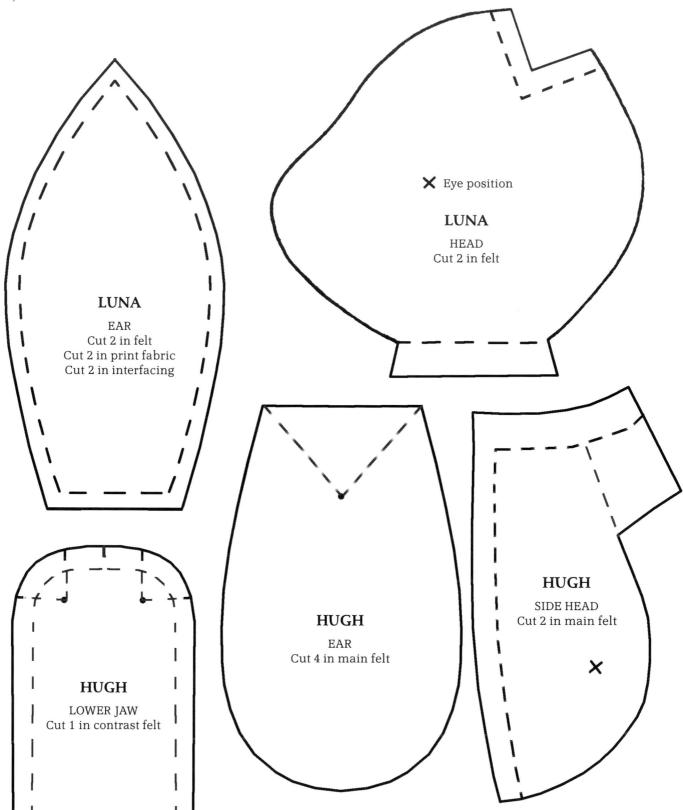

✘ Eye position

LUNA

HEAD
Cut 2 in felt

LUNA

EAR
Cut 2 in felt
Cut 2 in print fabric
Cut 2 in interfacing

HUGH

EAR
Cut 4 in main felt

HUGH

SIDE HEAD
Cut 2 in main felt

HUGH

LOWER JAW
Cut 1 in contrast felt

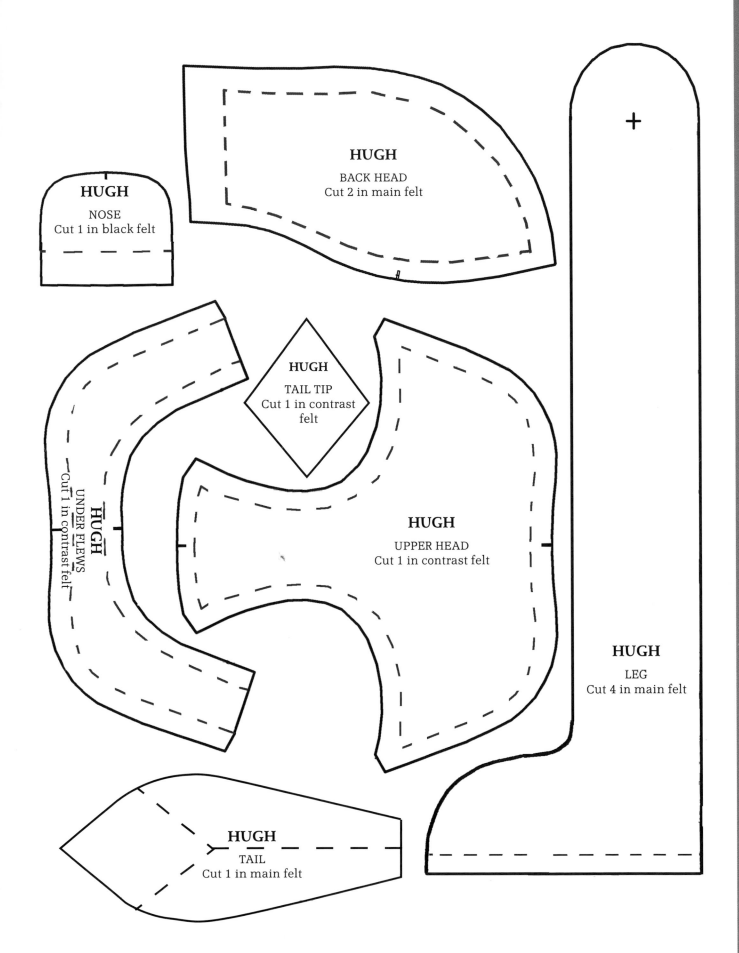

HUGH

NOSE
Cut 1 in black felt

HUGH

BACK HEAD
Cut 2 in main felt

HUGH

TAIL TIP
Cut 1 in contrast
felt

UNDER FLEWS
Cut 1 in contrast felt

HUGH

HUGH

UPPER HEAD
Cut 1 in contrast felt

HUGH

LEG
Cut 4 in main felt

HUGH

TAIL
Cut 1 in main felt

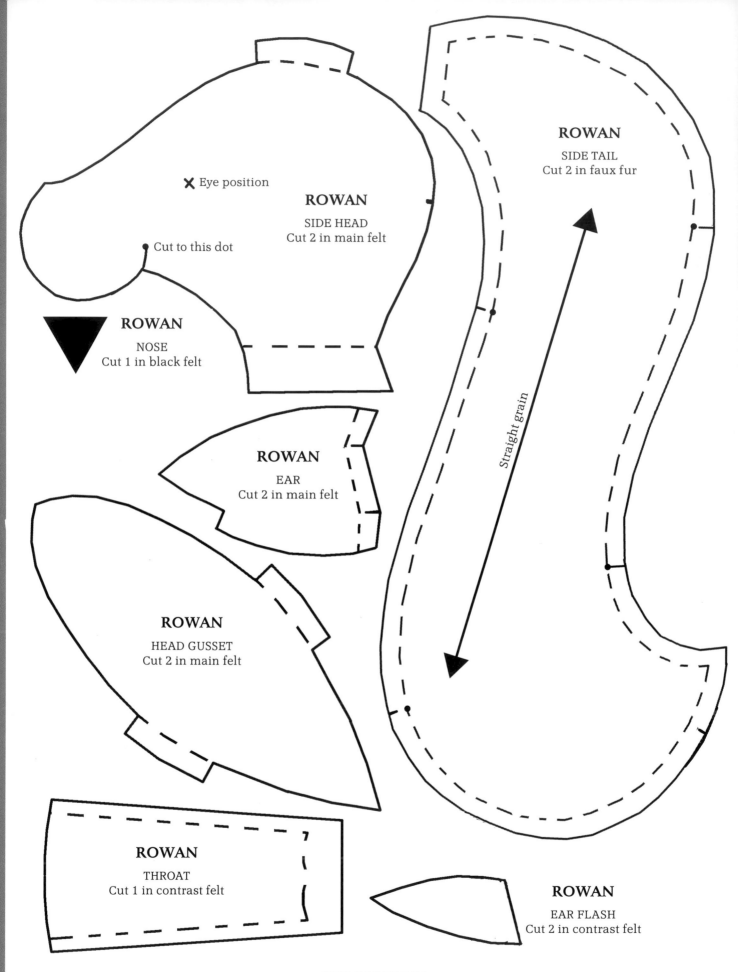

✗ Eye position

ROWAN

SIDE HEAD
Cut 2 in main felt

● Cut to this dot

ROWAN

NOSE
Cut 1 in black felt

ROWAN

SIDE TAIL
Cut 2 in faux fur

Straight grain

ROWAN

EAR
Cut 2 in main felt

ROWAN

HEAD GUSSET
Cut 2 in main felt

ROWAN

THROAT
Cut 1 in contrast felt

ROWAN

EAR FLASH
Cut 2 in contrast felt

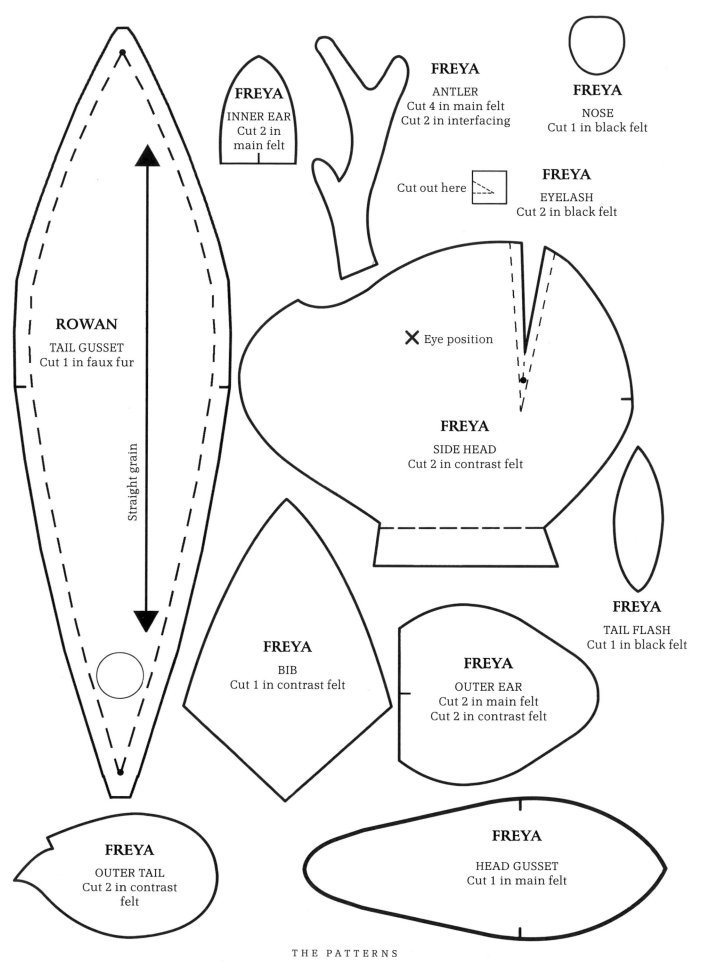

ROWAN

TAIL GUSSET
Cut 1 in faux fur

Straight grain

FREYA

INNER EAR
Cut 2 in
main felt

FREYA

ANTLER
Cut 4 in main felt
Cut 2 in interfacing

FREYA

NOSE
Cut 1 in black felt

Cut out here

FREYA

EYELASH
Cut 2 in black felt

✗ Eye position

FREYA

SIDE HEAD
Cut 2 in contrast felt

FREYA

TAIL FLASH
Cut 1 in black felt

FREYA

BIB
Cut 1 in contrast felt

FREYA

OUTER EAR
Cut 2 in main felt
Cut 2 in contrast felt

FREYA

OUTER TAIL
Cut 2 in contrast
felt

FREYA

HEAD GUSSET
Cut 1 in main felt

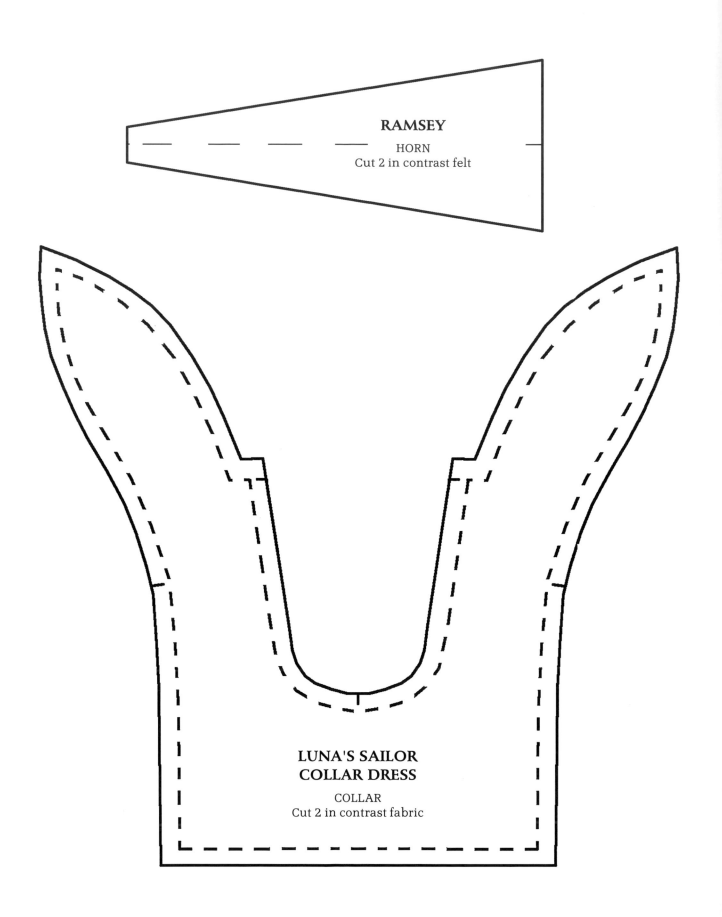

RAMSEY

HORN
Cut 2 in contrast felt

**LUNA'S SAILOR
COLLAR DRESS**

COLLAR
Cut 2 in contrast fabric

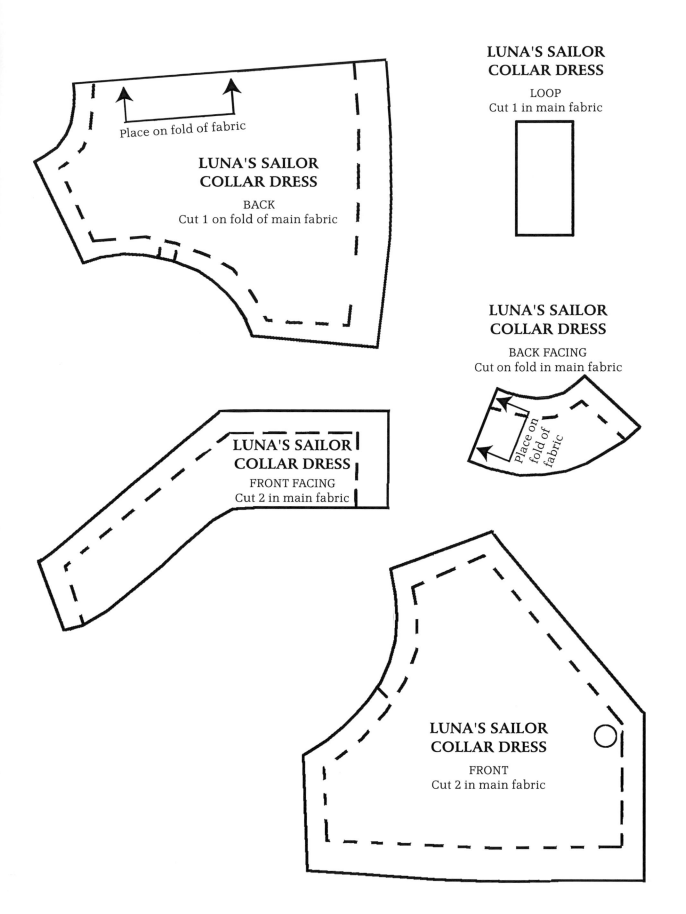

LUNA'S SAILOR
COLLAR DRESS

LOOP
Cut 1 in main fabric

Place on fold of fabric

LUNA'S SAILOR
COLLAR DRESS

BACK
Cut 1 on fold of main fabric

LUNA'S SAILOR
COLLAR DRESS

BACK FACING
Cut on fold in main fabric

Place on fold of fabric

LUNA'S SAILOR
COLLAR DRESS

FRONT FACING
Cut 2 in main fabric

LUNA'S SAILOR
COLLAR DRESS

FRONT
Cut 2 in main fabric

A

**LUNA'S SAILOR
COLLAR DRESS**

SKIRT
Join at Points A and B to complete pattern piece
Cut 1 on fold of main fabric

B

A

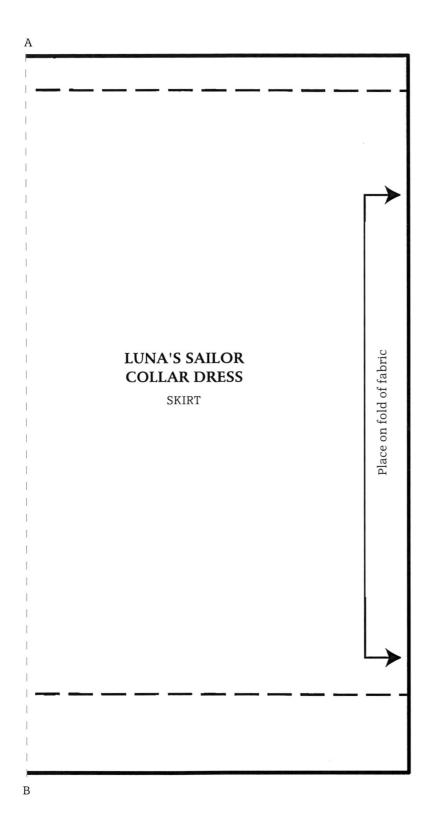

**LUNA'S SAILOR
COLLAR DRESS**

SKIRT

Place on fold of fabric

B

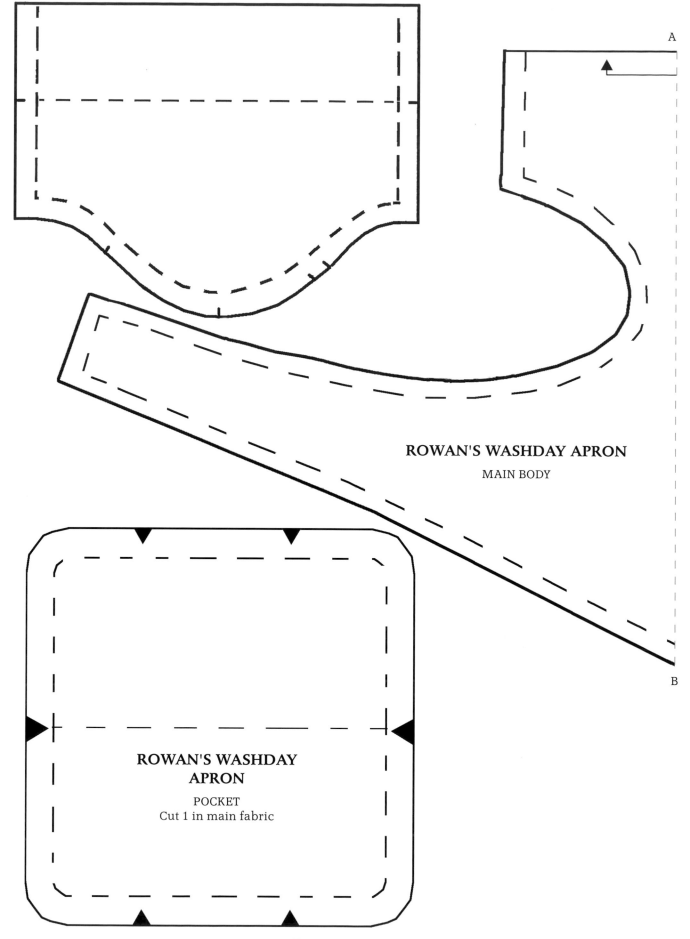

A

ROWAN'S WASHDAY APRON

MAIN BODY

B

ROWAN'S WASHDAY
APRON

POCKET
Cut 1 in main fabric

A

Place on fold of fabric

ROWAN'S WASHDAY APRON

MAIN BODY
Join at Points A and B to complete pattern piece
Cut 2 on fold in main fabric
(1 for outer and 1 for lining)

B

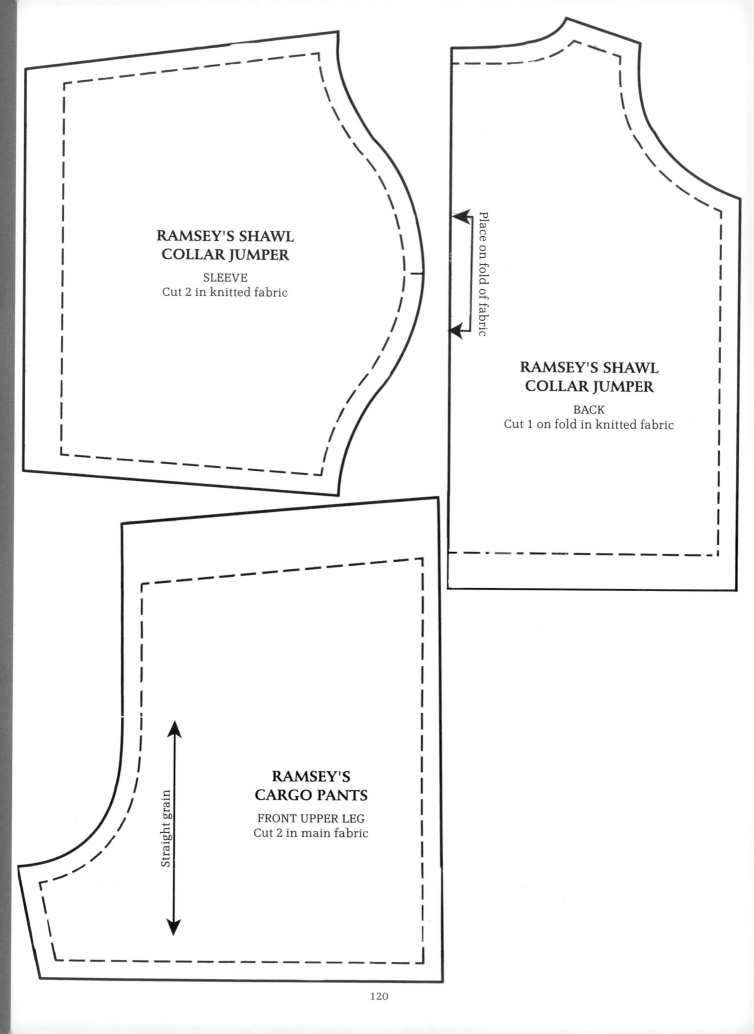

RAMSEY'S SHAWL COLLAR JUMPER

SLEEVE
Cut 2 in knitted fabric

Place on fold of fabric

RAMSEY'S SHAWL COLLAR JUMPER

BACK
Cut 1 on fold in knitted fabric

RAMSEY'S CARGO PANTS

FRONT UPPER LEG
Cut 2 in main fabric

Straight grain

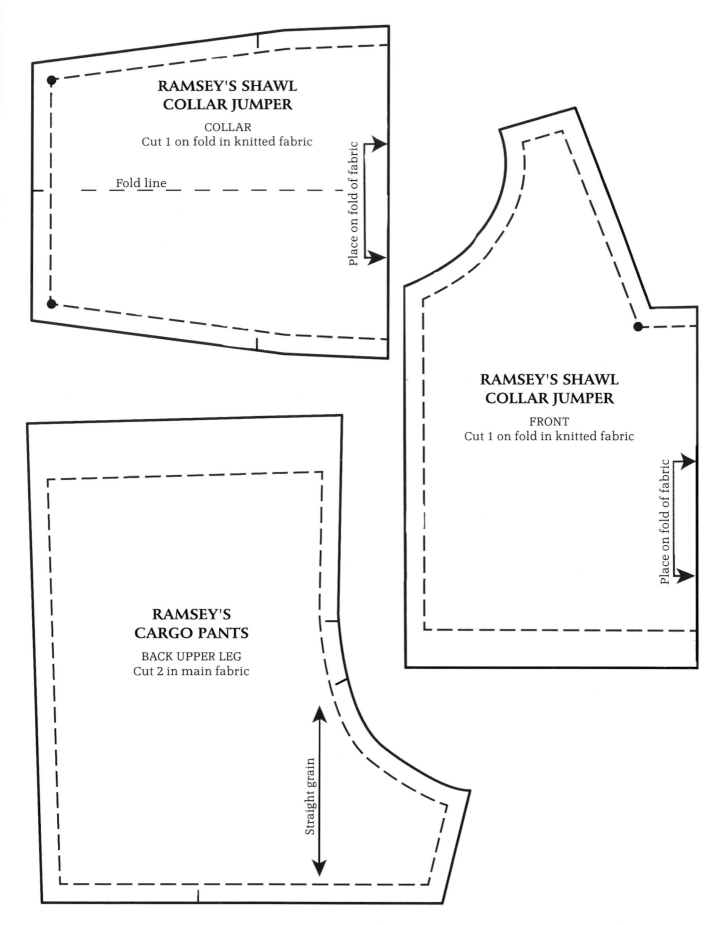

RAMSEY'S SHAWL COLLAR JUMPER

COLLAR
Cut 1 on fold in knitted fabric

Fold line

Place on fold of fabric

RAMSEY'S SHAWL COLLAR JUMPER

FRONT
Cut 1 on fold in knitted fabric

Place on fold of fabric

RAMSEY'S CARGO PANTS

BACK UPPER LEG
Cut 2 in main fabric

Straight grain

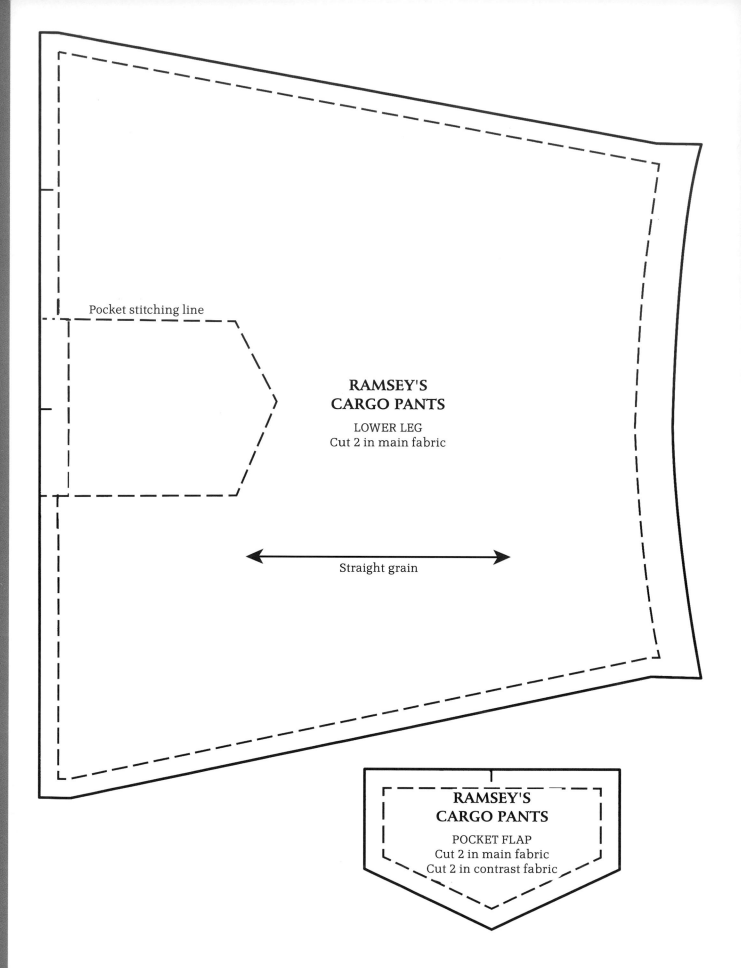

Pocket stitching line

**RAMSEY'S
CARGO PANTS**

LOWER LEG
Cut 2 in main fabric

Straight grain

**RAMSEY'S
CARGO PANTS**

POCKET FLAP
Cut 2 in main fabric
Cut 2 in contrast fabric

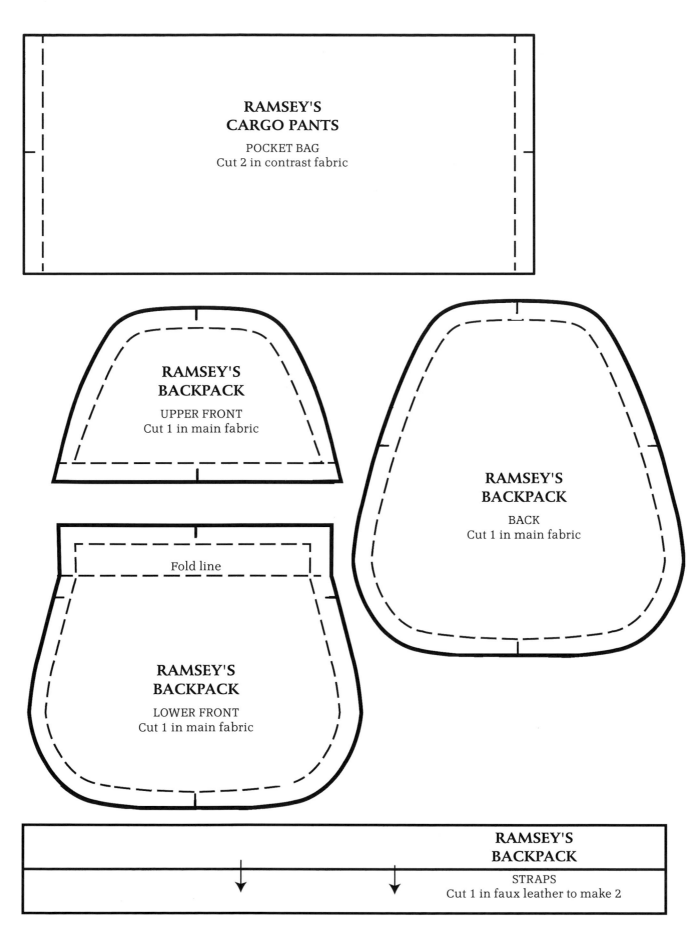

RAMSEY'S CARGO PANTS

POCKET BAG
Cut 2 in contrast fabric

RAMSEY'S BACKPACK

UPPER FRONT
Cut 1 in main fabric

RAMSEY'S BACKPACK

BACK
Cut 1 in main fabric

Fold line

RAMSEY'S BACKPACK

LOWER FRONT
Cut 1 in main fabric

RAMSEY'S BACKPACK

STRAPS
Cut 1 in faux leather to make 2

RAMSEY'S BACKPACK

UNDERBAND
Cut 1 in main fabric

DAISY'S TWIRLING DRESS

POCKET STITCHING TEMPLATE

A

B

A

DAISY'S TWIRLING DRESS

SKIRT
Join at Points A and B to complete pattern piece
Cut 2 on fold in main fabric
Cut 2 on fold in dress net

B

RAMSEY'S BACKPACK

ZIP EDGE STRIPS
Cut 1 in main fabric to make 2

A

place in fold of fabric

DAISY'S TWIRLING
DRESS

SKIRT

B

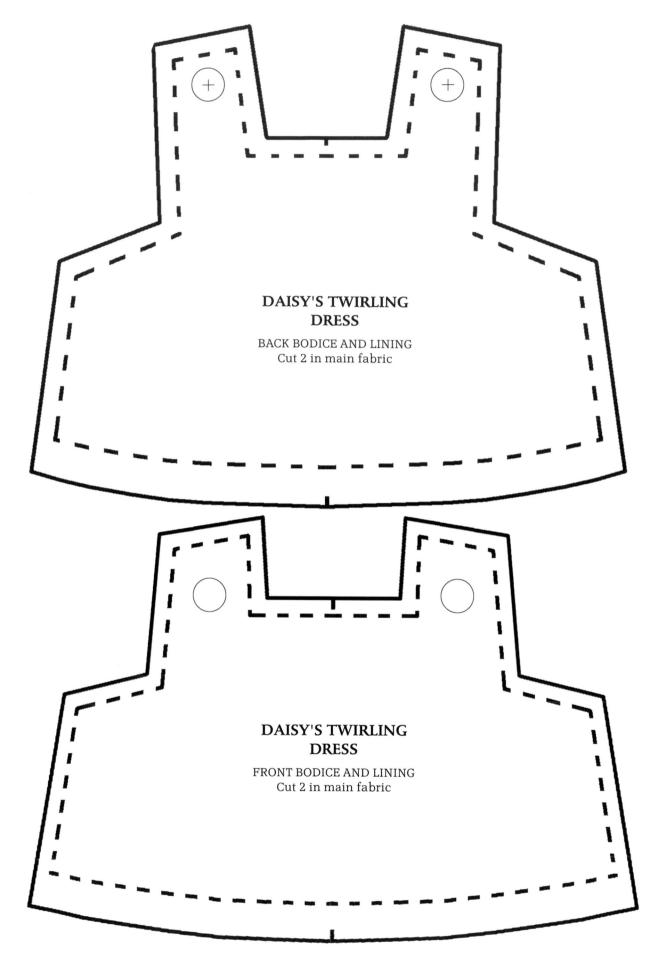

DAISY'S TWIRLING DRESS

BACK BODICE AND LINING
Cut 2 in main fabric

DAISY'S TWIRLING DRESS

FRONT BODICE AND LINING
Cut 2 in main fabric

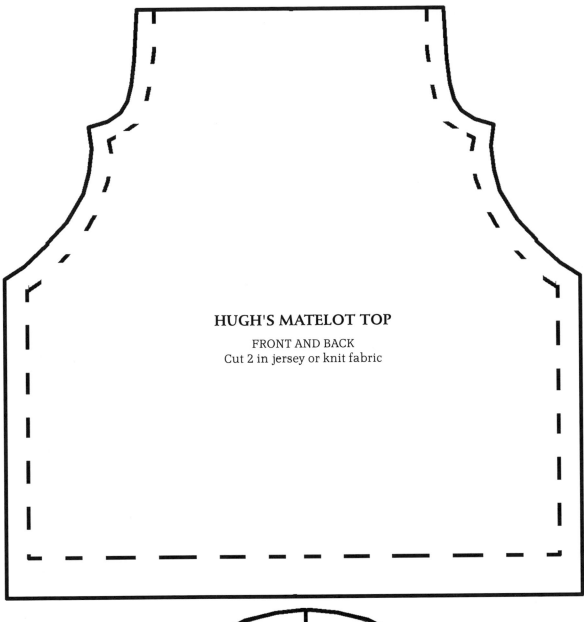

HUGH'S MATELOT TOP

FRONT AND BACK
Cut 2 in jersey or knit fabric

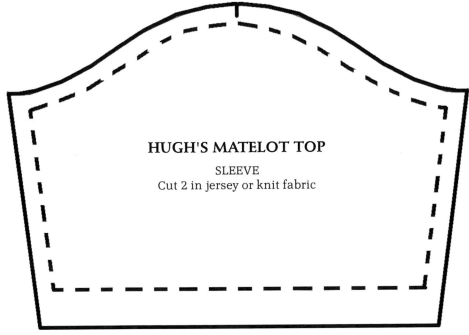

HUGH'S MATELOT TOP

SLEEVE
Cut 2 in jersey or knit fabric

HUGH'S BUTTON-FRONT TROUSERS

BACK FACING
Cut 1 in main fabric

HUGH'S BANDANA

BANDANA
Cut 1 on fold in main fabric

Place on fold of fabric

HUGH'S BUTTON-FRONT TROUSERS

FRONT FACING
Cut 1 in main fabric

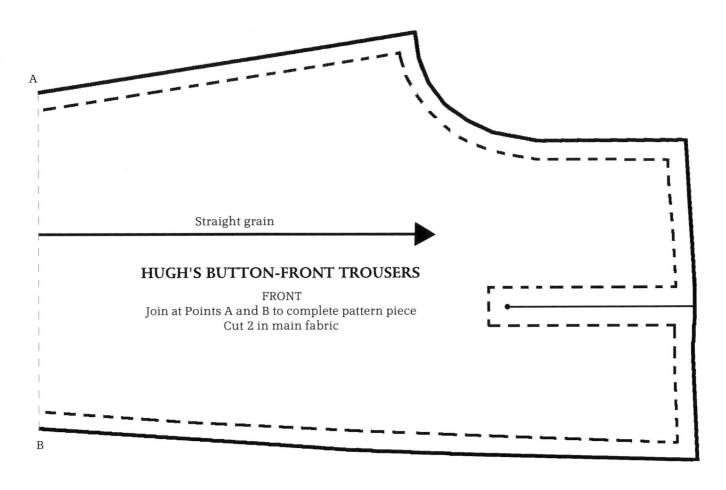

Straight grain

HUGH'S BUTTON-FRONT TROUSERS

FRONT
Join at Points A and B to complete pattern piece
Cut 2 in main fabric

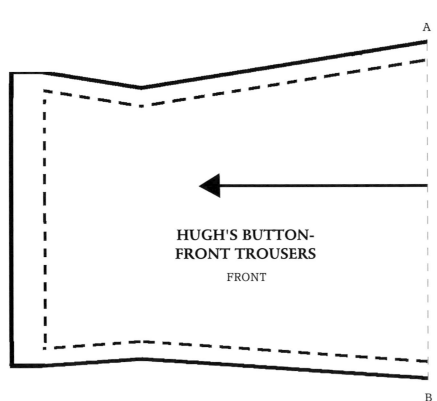

HUGH'S BUTTON-FRONT TROUSERS

FRONT

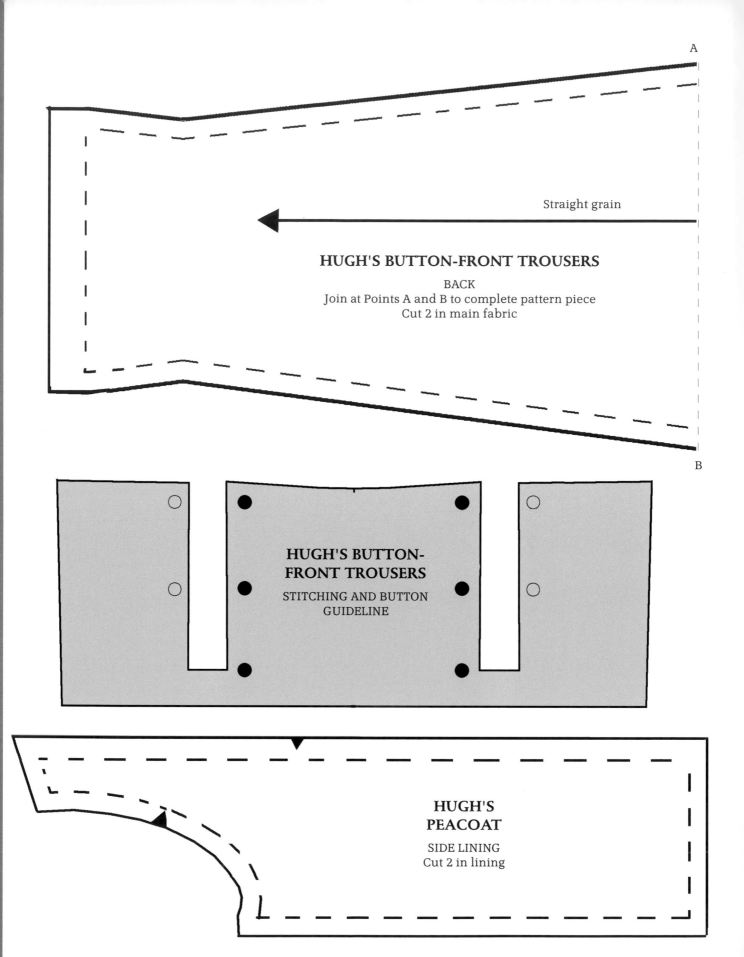

A

Straight grain

HUGH'S BUTTON-FRONT TROUSERS

BACK
Join at Points A and B to complete pattern piece
Cut 2 in main fabric

B

**HUGH'S BUTTON-
FRONT TROUSERS**

STITCHING AND BUTTON
GUIDELINE

**HUGH'S
PEACOAT**

SIDE LINING
Cut 2 in lining

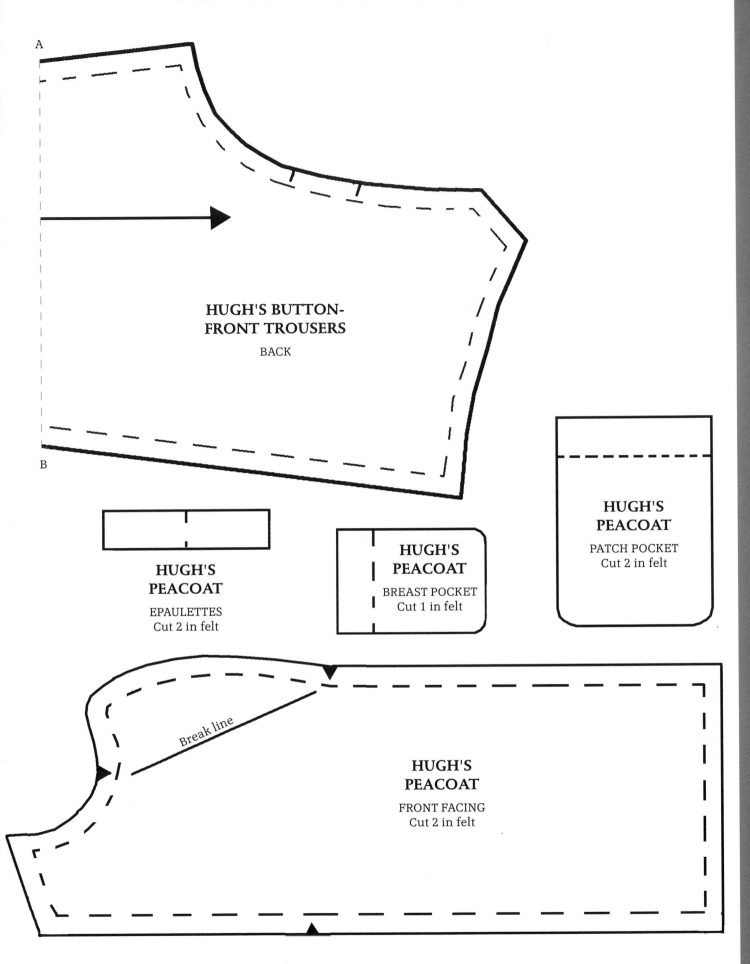

A

B

HUGH'S BUTTON-FRONT TROUSERS

BACK

HUGH'S PEACOAT

EPAULETTES
Cut 2 in felt

HUGH'S PEACOAT

BREAST POCKET
Cut 1 in felt

HUGH'S PEACOAT

PATCH POCKET
Cut 2 in felt

Break line

HUGH'S PEACOAT

FRONT FACING
Cut 2 in felt

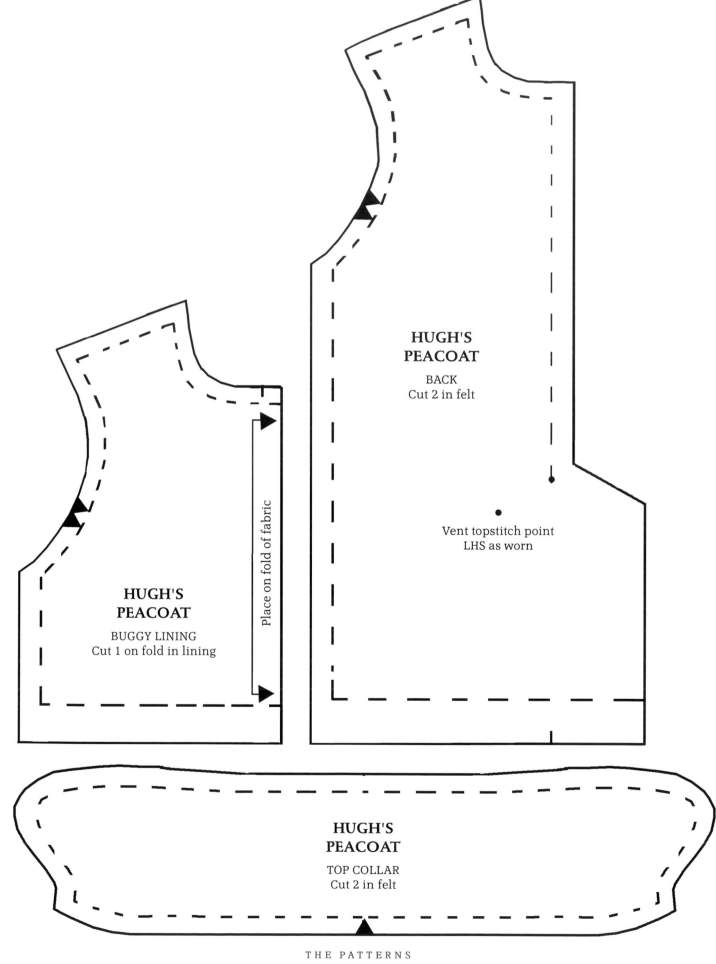

HUGH'S PEACOAT

BACK
Cut 2 in felt

Vent topstitch point
LHS as worn

Place on fold of fabric

HUGH'S PEACOAT

BUGGY LINING
Cut 1 on fold in lining

HUGH'S PEACOAT

TOP COLLAR
Cut 2 in felt

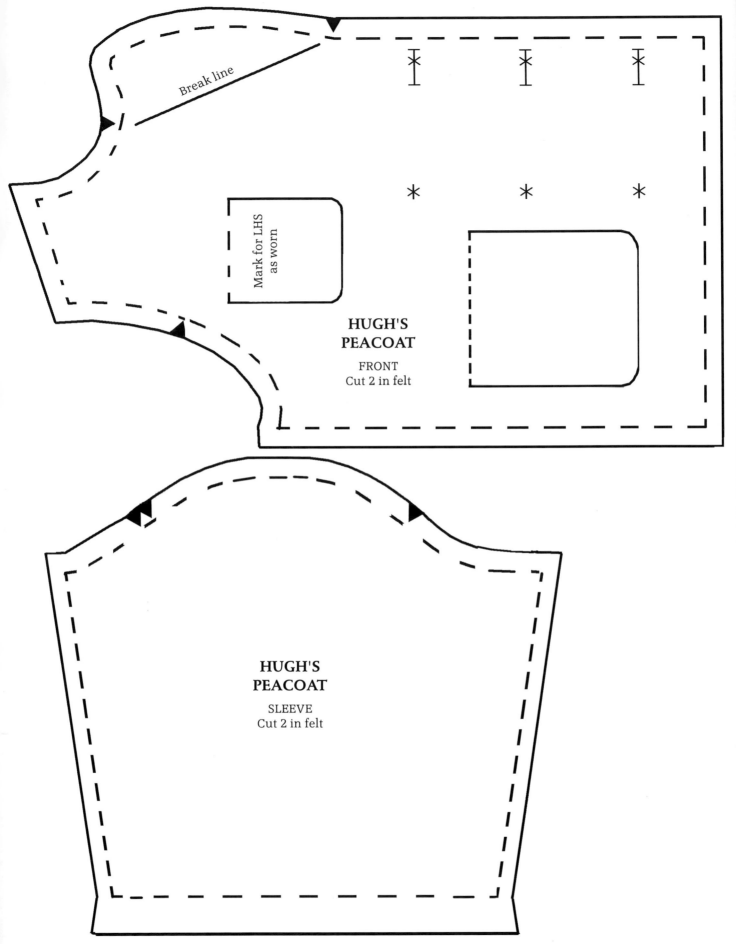

Break line

Mark for LHS as worn

HUGH'S PEACOAT

FRONT
Cut 2 in felt

HUGH'S PEACOAT

SLEEVE
Cut 2 in felt

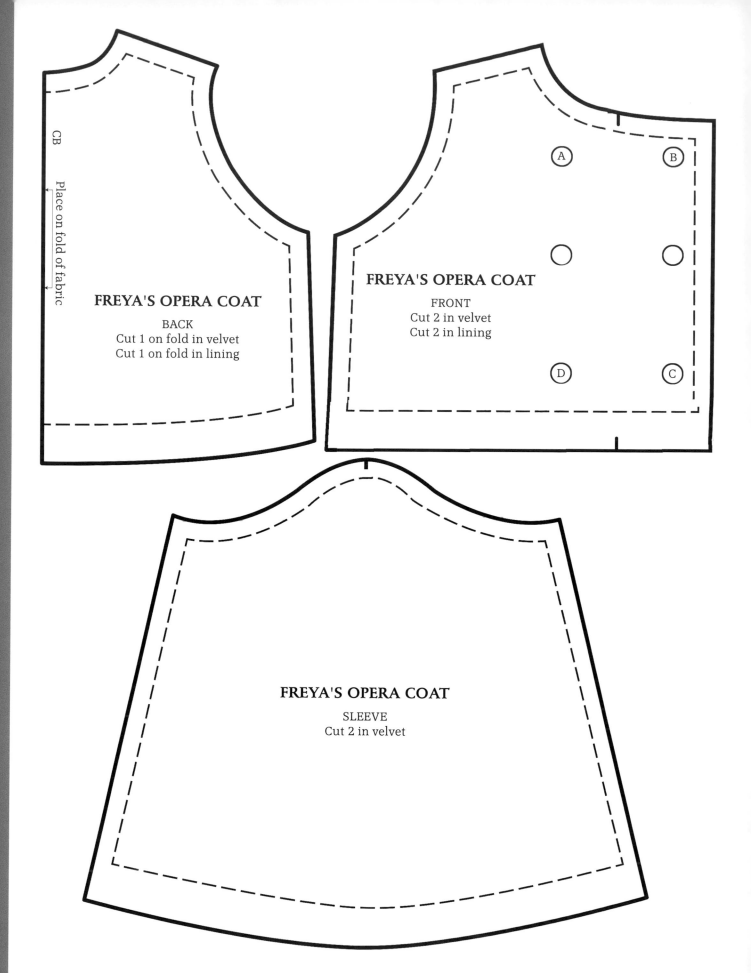

FREYA'S OPERA COAT

BACK
Cut 1 on fold in velvet
Cut 1 on fold in lining

CB

Place on fold of fabric

FREYA'S OPERA COAT

FRONT
Cut 2 in velvet
Cut 2 in lining

Ⓐ   Ⓑ

○   ○

Ⓓ   Ⓒ

FREYA'S OPERA COAT

SLEEVE
Cut 2 in velvet

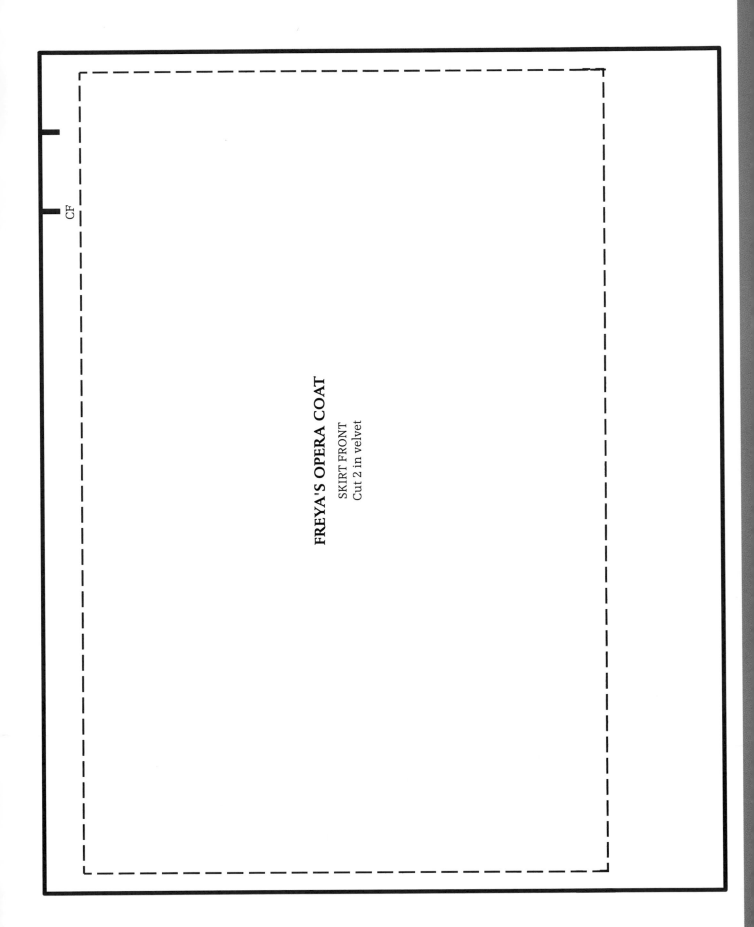

FREYA'S OPERA COAT

SKIRT FRONT
Cut 2 in velvet

CF

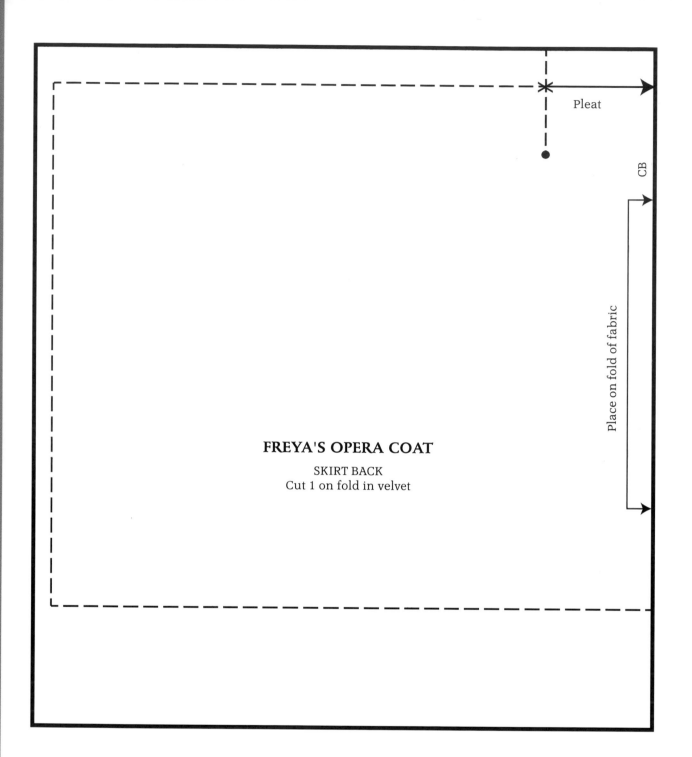

Pleat

CB

Place on fold of fabric

FREYA'S OPERA COAT

SKIRT BACK
Cut 1 on fold in velvet

FREYA'S MUSIC SATCHEL

FLAP STRAPS
Cut 2 in felt

FREYA'S MUSIC SATCHEL

POCKET
Cut 1 in felt

FREYA'S MUSIC SATCHEL

FLAP
Cut 1 in felt

FREYA'S MUSIC SATCHEL

FRONT AND BACK
Cut 2 in felt

FREYA'S MUSIC SATCHEL

GUSSET
Cut 1 in felt

FREYA'S MUSIC SATCHEL

BODY STRAP
Cut 1 in felt

Pleat

Place on fold of fabric

Straight grain

A

B

FREYA'S HALTERNECK PLAYSUIT

SKIRT
Join at Points A and B to complete pattern piece
Cut 1 on fold in taffeta

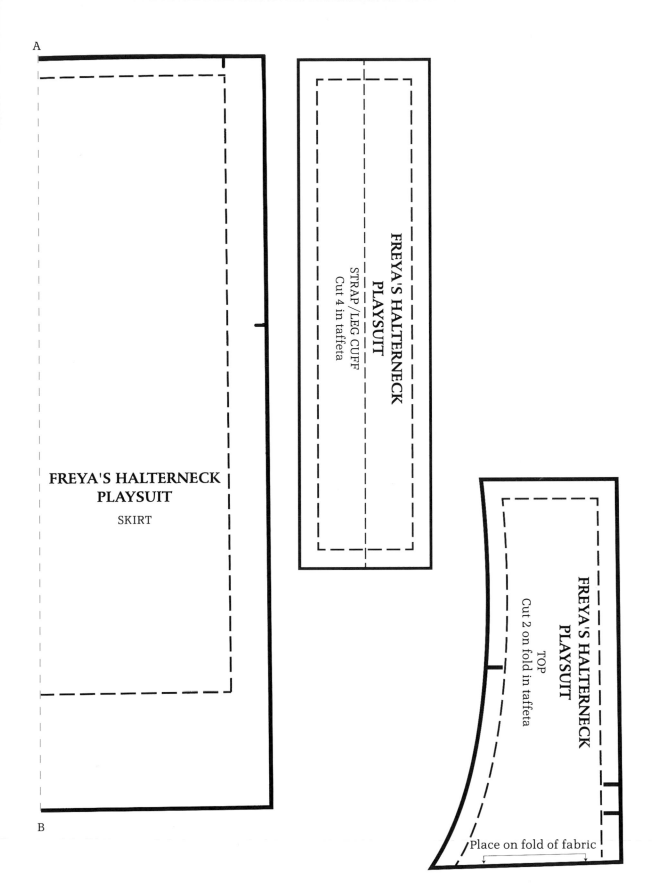

A

FREYA'S HALTERNECK PLAYSUIT

SKIRT

B

FREYA'S HALTERNECK PLAYSUIT

STRAP / LEG CUFF

Cut 4 in taffeta

FREYA'S HALTERNECK PLAYSUIT

TOP

Cut 2 on fold in taffeta

Place on fold of fabric

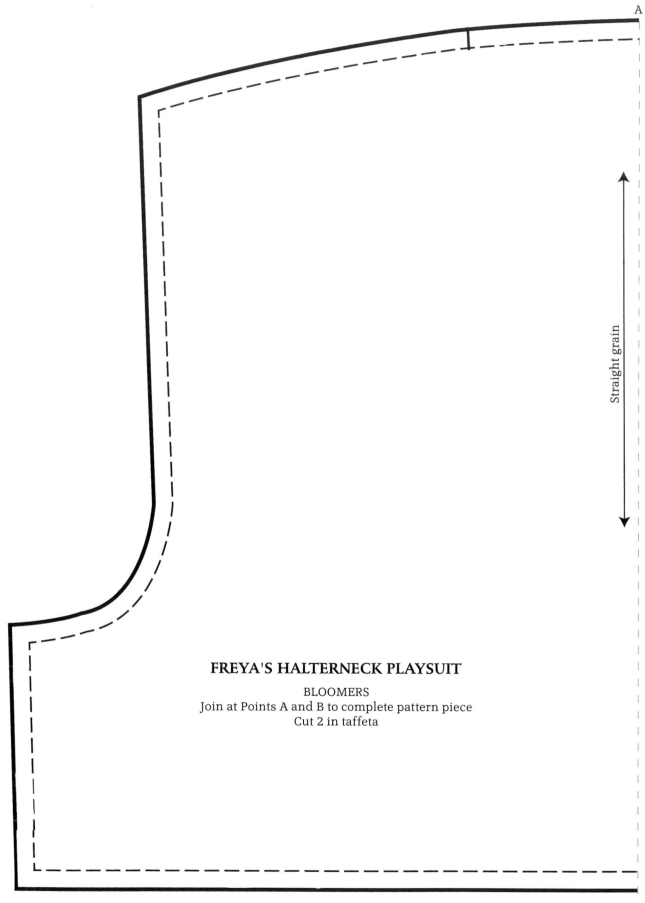

A

Straight grain

FREYA'S HALTERNECK PLAYSUIT

BLOOMERS
Join at Points A and B to complete pattern piece
Cut 2 in taffeta

B

A

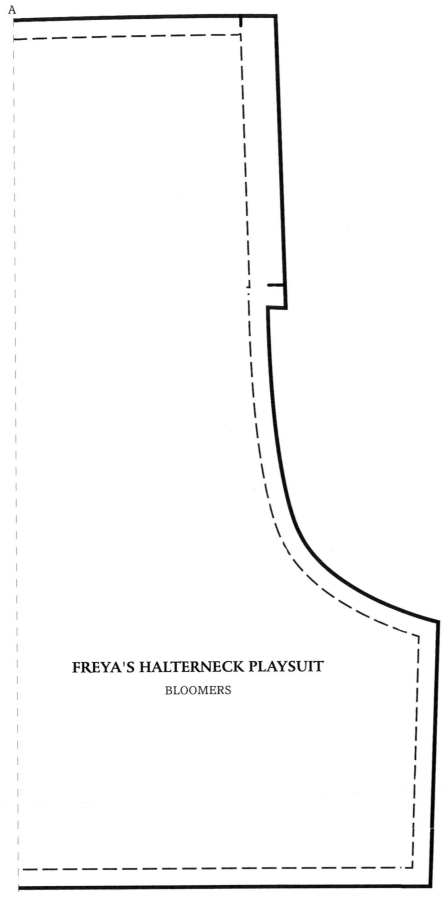

FREYA'S HALTERNECK PLAYSUIT

BLOOMERS

B

Suppliers

Think first, what do you already have? It might not be exactly as we have prescribed, but will it do the job, will it improve the job, will it bring an undefinable element of 'your story' to the end project? If you are wanting these pieces to mean more, try to incorporate little bits of your life into them. It could be a 'past its best' shirt or an old pair of leather gloves – but tiny amounts can equal tiny clothes and accessories. While I would encourage you to let your imagination go to work on the clothes, I would advise that you use the best felt you can for the animal characters themselves. If you fancy something specific, do support your local fabric experts – the little haberdasheries on the high street who need you to shop with them – even if it's just for the odd bobbin of thread or a fat quarter. Big supermarket chains don't care about fabric, they haven't chosen the prints with excitement or love. Shop local, shop small. Speaking of which…

COOLCRAFTING – HOME OF LUNA LAPIN

The shop for everything featured in this book – kits, remake kits, felt, Liberty prints, tiny buckles and buttons, and all the latest Luna frippery. Worldwide shipping.
7 Stramongate
Kendal
Cumbria
LA94BH
Tel: 01539 724099
Email: info@coolcrafting.co.uk
Website: www.coolcrafting.co.uk

About the Author

Sarah Peel is the founder of CoolCrafting, a business established in 2011 to deliver crafting and sewing inspiration. Today, the business is primarily driven by Luna Lapin and her growing set of friends. With a team of ten staff, CoolCrafting is homed in the oldest existing shop in the historic town of Kendal, Cumbria. Luna lovers from all over the country can make a pilgrimage to the Home of Luna, to shop and learn at friendly workshops.

With a background in fashion pattern cutting, womenswear design and buying, Sarah's ultimate aim is to move you on from making beautiful clothes for Luna to making your own clothes! Sarah and her team have a busy website and, as well as supplying kits for the miniature characters, the business provides contemporary dressmaking supplies and yarns for the modern handmade wardrobe.

Sarah lives on the edge of the English Lake District in Hincaster, Cumbria, with her partner Anthony. Occasionally, her three grown up children live in the rather untidy house too, along with rescue dog Harvey. Sarah's daughter Grace has written beautiful stories for Luna, many of which reflect tiny nuggets of their real family and business life.

To find out more about the CoolCrafting business go to www.coolcrafting.co.uk or join us on Facebook at Luna Lapin's Little World.

Acknowledgements

More than anyone else, I would like to acknowledge the support of the creative Luna Lapin community, the (mainly) women who send me kind messages when I am beyond tired, who share their ideas and makes, and who support and lift one another up with endless good-natured advice.

To my fabulous CoolCrafting team of strong, inspirational, hardworking 'girls', who I can rely on to keep things running when one of my many life disasters happens.

Of course, I want to thank my family for seeing me through the painful start-up years. To my mum, Joan, who taught me to sew, who gave me the ability to see that petals and leaves could become dresses for tiny garden fairies, that our dolls might be alive whilst we slept and, even in later life, that there are animals who talk and mice who steal your spectacles.

I would also like to thank Cheryl Brown for working on editing and improving my work within this book in such a thorough and professional manner.

Index

antlers 102–3, 113
apron, Rowan's washday 22–5, 118–19
arms 79, 85, 97–8, 106, 108

backpacks 35–7, 123–5
backstitch 9
bags 35–7, 72–3, 123–5, 137
bandanas 59, 128
blanket stitch 9
bloomers 63–6, 140–1
bodices 17–18, 40–2, 63, 66
bodies 78–9, 84, 90, 97, 104–5, 107–8
broderie anglaise 42–3
buttonholes 11, 58
buttons 18, 43, 51, 58, 71, 79, 82, 91, 95, 104

cargo pants 31–4, 120–3
coats 52–8, 67–71, 130–6
collars 14–16, 18, 28–30, 56, 120–1, 132
corduroy 6, 31–4
corners, turning 10
cotton 14–19, 22–5, 57
crotches 64–5
cuffs 63–4
curves 10, 22–3
cutting out 8, 106
    accessories 22, 35, 59
    clothing 14, 28, 31, 40, 46, 48, 52, 62, 67
    dolls 76, 80, 86, 92, 99, 101

D rings 37
Daisy the Sheep 38, 60, 74
    doll pattern 92–8, 99–100, 107–9
    twirling dress 40–3, 124–6
donkeys (stitch starters) 10
dresses 14–19, 40–3, 114–18, 124–6

ears 76–7, 80–7, 93, 102–3, 106–13
easing 10
edgestitches 11
elasticated waists 50–1
embroidery 9, 79, 95
epaulettes 55, 131
eyes 79, 82, 91, 95, 104, 113

fabrics 6–7
    right side/wrong side 8
faux fur 7
faux leather (pleather) 7, 35–7
feet 78, 84, 96, 107, 109
felt 6, 35–7, 52–8, 72–3, 76–105

Freya the Fawn 60–73, 74
    doll pattern 101–5, 106–7, 113
    halterneck playsuit 62–6, 138–41
    music satchel 72–3, 137
    opera coat 67–71, 134–5

gathers 11, 17, 42, 63–5, 68, 70
grainlines 106

halterneck playsuit 62–6, 138–41
hand sewing stitches 8–9
hand wheels 10
heads 77, 81–3, 87–90, 93–5, 100–7, 109–13
hems 18, 30, 34, 51, 57, 71
horns 99–100, 114
Hugh Houndslow 44–59, 60, 74
    bandana 59, 128
    button-front trousers 48–51, 128–31
    doll pattern 80–5, 106–8, 110–11
    Matelot top 46–7, 127
    peacoat 52–8, 130–3

jersey fabrics 6, 28–30, 46–7
jumper, Ramsey's shawl collar 28–30, 120–1

knitted fabrics 6, 28–30

layout diagrams 8
legs
    doll 78, 84–5, 96–8, 107, 109, 111
    trouser 31–4, 51, 63–6
    linings 22–4, 31–2, 40–1, 52, 54–7, 68–9
Luna Lapin 12–19, 20, 26, 38, 44, 60, 74
    doll pattern 76–9, 106–7, 110
    sailor collar dress 14–19, 114–18

machine sewing techniques 10–11
materials 6–7

needlefelt technique 104, 105
noses 79, 82, 89, 95, 104, 111, 113

opera coat 67–71, 134–6
overstitch (whipstitch) 8

patterns 8, 106–41
peacoat 52–8, 130–3
playsuit, halterneck 62–6, 138–41
pleats 23, 65–6, 67
pockets 22–3, 32–3, 43, 53, 72, 131

press studs 43, 51, 66, 71, 73, 91
pressing techniques 11
printed fabrics 6, 8

Ramsey the Ram 26–37, 38, 74
    backpack 35–7, 123–5
    cargo pants 31–4, 120–3
    doll pattern 99–100, 107–9, 114
    shawl collar jumper 28–30, 120–1
    raw edges, finishing 8
Rowan Redtail the Squirrel 20–6, 74
    doll pattern 86–91, 106–7, 112–13
    washday apron 22–5, 118–19

satchel, music 72–3, 137
satin stitch 9
seam allowances 10
securing stitches 10
sewing kits 6
shoulder seams 15, 28, 54–5, 68
side seams 17, 30–2, 41–2, 47, 50, 57, 71
skirts 17–18, 41–3, 65–8, 70–1, 116–17, 124–5, 135–6, 138–9
sleeves 16–17, 29, 47, 57, 69, 127, 133–4
slip stitch (ladder stitch) 9
spots 105
staystitching 10
stitches 8–10
straps 23–4, 62–3, 66, 72–3, 123, 137, 139

taffeta 7, 62–71
tails 79, 85, 90–1, 98, 105, 111–13
techniques 8–11
toggles 18
top, Hugh's Matelot 46–7, 127
topstitches 11
transferring markings 8
trims 42–3
trousers 31–4, 48–51, 63–6, 120–3, 128–31, 140–1
turnups 51

underarms 17, 47

velvet 7, 67–71
vents 53–4, 58

waist casings 34
waists, elasticated 50–1

zip loops 35–7

A DAVID AND CHARLES BOOK
© David and Charles, Ltd 2020

David and Charles is an imprint of David and Charles, Ltd
Suite A, Tourism House, Pynes Hill, Exeter, EX2 5WT

First published in the UK and USA in 2020

A catalogue record for this book is available from the British Library.

ISBN-13: 9781446308240 paperback
ISBN-13: 9781446379790 EPUB

Printed in the UK by Pureprint for:
David and Charles, Ltd
Suite A, Tourism House, Pynes Hill, Exeter, EX2 5WT

10 9 8 7 6 5 4 3 2

Senior Commissioning Editor: Sarah Callard
Managing Editor: Jessica Cropper
Project Editor: Cheryl Brown
Head of Design: Anna Wade
Art Direction, Layout and Design: Prudence Rogers
Pre-press Designer: Ali Stark
Photographer: Jason Jenkins
Production Manager: Beverley Richardson

David and Charles publishes high-quality books on a wide range of subjects.
For more information visit www.davidandcharles.com.

Luna Lapin

MAKING NEW FRIENDS

Sewing patterns from Luna's little world

Sarah Peel
With short stories by Grace Machon